I0521162

Headhunter

www.stickingplacebooks.com

© Cynthia Costa Cohen 2025
Cover design © Maria Wilk
Introduction © James Kenney
© Sticking Place Books 2025

ISBN 979-8-89976-032-7

Headhunter

A screenplay by
Larry Cohen

Sticking Place Books
New York

Prescription for Chaos
Headhunter and the Films (and Fantasies) of Larry Cohen

by James Kenney

"My pictures are mine. Individual and special."

> Larry Cohen, interviewed by
> Maitland McDonagh,
> *Columbia Film Review*

"When I write, I'm watching the movie in my head, imagining it. I want to be in it. I don't like to see words I'm writing."

> Larry Cohen, quoted by Amy Wallace
> in *The New Yorker*

"My basic education was going to the movies... I just assimilated it. I knew structure and form and just inherently could do it…. If you can jump in at an interesting situation with interesting characters and let them take you for a ride, and allow the characters to come to life, then you can't wait to get back to writing the next day because you'll be excited at where they take you."

> Larry Cohen, in *Screenwriters Monthly*

Filmmaker Larry Cohen's name is less familiar to the general public than to critics and aficionados of cult cinema, yet to those attuned to his work's subversive power and rough-hewn vitality, he endures as one of the medium's most inventive figures, conjuring mutant infants, winged serpents, and killer desserts into narratives that operate at once as pulp spectacle and as sharp critiques of contemporary society. His flair for provocation extended beyond the screen. In mid-1970s London, Cohen had baby carriages roll through Piccadilly Circus, each marked with a sign that read, "If you want to see the baby, you've got to go and see *It's Alive.*" Shoppers were startled to hear demonic infant growls from inside the carriages, a bit of carnival ballyhoo that was pure Cohen: humorous, shocking, and wholly in service to his art. He might bait you with William Castle-style stunts to see his film, but the twist was that it's a genuinely great film.

Cohen carved a renegade path, cutting his teeth as a teenage stand-up comedian, then muscling into television in the 1960s with scripts for *The Defenders* and creating the *X-Files* precursor *The Invaders.* From there he moved on to writing, producing, and directing theatrical features, ruling as a one-man-band auteur for two decades, banging out singular genre landmarks like *Black Caesar* and *Q: The Winged Serpent.* And as other writers' phones stopped ringing, Cohen's kept buzzing, when in his mid-sixties he reinvented himself as a well-compensated Hollywood gun-for-hire, penning the sleek studio thrillers *Phone Booth,* with Colin Farrell. Through it all, he remained the quintessential guerrilla filmmaker: unconventional, resourceful, never once weary of the hustle.

In an era when B-movies were dismissed as disreputable grindhouse fare, Cohen used them as his personal sandbox to play with big ideas. He smuggled social satire and sharp commentary into drive-in horror flicks and crime capers with titles like *Hell Up in Harlem* and *It Lives Again* (a sequel, naturally, to *It Lives*), pushing exploitation films into territory at once sharper and more daring than the market ever demanded. And he did it all with a mischievous grin and a truly eccentric flair.

Beneath the rubber creatures and explosive squib-laden shootouts, his films carried an undercurrent of meaning, a drive to engage with real conflicts and anxieties. Speaking to interviewer Geoffrey McNab, Cohen himself insisted, "I want the picture to be about something – not just action and

It's Alive.

violence." That insistence on significance marked Cohen as an anomalous figure within exploitation cinema, transforming disreputable forms into vessels for cultural provocation, collapsing the boundary between low-budget spectacle and serious cultural discourse. Even as his films unspooled as 42nd Street double features, they were simultaneously being subjected to rigorous deconstruction by no less than Robin Wood in *Film Comment*.

Cohen made low-budget genre films not because he was forced to, but because he loved them—relishing the freedom of style and subject matter denied to bigger-budgeted Hollywood productions. His work pulsed with anarchic vitality and a slyly mordant wit, fusing the garish with the deeply psychological, and grinding pulp into something sharper, more disquieting. On the surface, his films often begin with "high-concept" premises— a winged serpent attacking New York, unrelated strangers committing murder while muttering "God told me to," a hitman romancing the mother of a small child who witnessed a murder. Underneath such baroque spectacle lurked nightmares drawn directly from daily anxieties.

His films blend horror, comedy, and action, tackling topics like racism, abortion, consumerism, religion, and the American family – all articulated within the popular idioms of horror, science fiction and pulp violence.

Brash and self-assured, Cohen emerged as a rare triple threat—writer, producer, and director—driven by a restless imagination and a taste for provocation. In *The Invaders*, aliens disguise themselves as humans while only one man knows the truth (Cohen later called it "a parody of the McCarthy years, a witch hunt of aliens"), while *Branded* is a Western about a "blacklisted" cowboy, a conceit that earning the disapproval of right-wing star Chuck Connors. By the 1970s he had turned his energies toward cinema, staking out territory across a startling range of genres: Blaxploitation with *Black Caesar* (which he insisted was "a film about family life"); horror with *It's Alive* (Cohen to *Sight and Sound*: "I don't think *It's Alive* is more of a horror story than *The Elephant Man*"); paranoid science fiction in *God Told Me To* (where an alien is mistaken for a messiah, Cohen telling *The New Yorker* he was "inspired by America's emerging gay culture"); political exposé in *The Private Files of J. Edgar Hoover* (his answer to Jimmy Stewart's "whitewashed" *The F.B.I. Story*); and satiric black comedy in his directing debut *Bone*, an acerbic portrait of liberals scrambling to mask their own prejudices. As writer Tony Williams observed on the website *Senses of Cinema*, Cohen "utilized radical allegory" in *It's Alive* to mount an ironic critique of one of America's most cherished icons—the family. The film mobilized the horror genre as a site for exploring the psychic repressions of the nuclear family, exposing how parental anxieties about their children's differences or unpredictability can metastasize into nightmare. This kind of sneaky social commentary was Cohen's forte.

Cohen continued turning out uniquely offbeat films. In 1976 he gave the world *God Told Me To*, a provocative thriller in which random New Yorkers suddenly become spree killers, all claiming divine instruction. What begins as a crime mystery veers into science fiction and blasphemous

God Told Me To.

satire, encompassing Cohen's stunt of planting a young Andy Kaufman, in full police uniform, into the real New York City St. Patrick's Day parade, where he suddenly obeys God by pulling a gun and firing into the crowd as Cohen's cameras rolled. It wasn't only the content that defied convention but the form itself. Cohen shot with the same audacity that charged his stories—driving cabs onto sidewalks in midtown Manhattan, staging fistfights at the baggage claim in Los Angeles International Airport, hijacking public events as ready-made sets. The result was cinema that felt reckless and alive, its provocations inseparable from the way it was made.

By the 1980s, Cohen's bravado had become so conspicuous it was making headlines. *Q: The Winged Serpent* turned the Chrysler Building into his personal backlot, complete with phony NYPD officers led by David Carradine firing machine guns from its turret high above Midtown, a spectacle that collapsed the line between cinematic fantasy and urban reality, resulting in *New York Post* headlines and admonishment from Mayor Ed Koch. Cohen followed it with *The Stuff* (tagline: "Are you eating

it, or is it eating you?"), a satirical horror film in which the allegory is scarcely disguised: consumers eagerly embrace a substance that consumes them in turn, a junk-food monstrosity extending Cohen's critique of American appetites into the terrain of body horror.

Throughout the decade, Cohen kept commandeering Manhattan as his stage, turning out scrappy indies like *Perfect Strangers* and *Special Effects*, utilizing local counterculture figures like Eric Bogosian *(Talk Radio)*, Zoë Tamerlis *(Ms. 45)*, and Ann Carlisle *(Liquid Sky)* as his leads. At the same time, he cultivated a reputation for professional volatility, deliberately getting himself fired from higher-budget assignments such as *I, the Jury* — where he admitted he had planned to subvert Mickey Spillane's Mike Hammer — and *Deadly Illusion*, since quitting outright would have left him open to lawsuits. Both films suffered fatally in his absence, their strongest moments all traceable to Cohen's characteristic, original scripts.

Commentators often remarked on the ferocity of Cohen's vision. In the late 1970s, Robin Wood argued that "the work of Larry Cohen...does not offer an alternative, except by implication, to a society perceived as locked in the processes of its own self-destruction." For Wood, even films dismissed by mainstream critics revealed unexpected depth: *It's Alive*, widely written off as a "*Rosemary's Baby–Exorcist* rip-off," was, in his view, "more intelligent than either, and owes them about as much as *Rio Bravo* owes *High Noon*." Regarding *God Told Me To*, Wood observed that "the issues it opens up are both immense and profound, and absolutely central to our culture and its future development."

Throughout his career, other critics echoed this sense of Cohen as a filmmaker whose pulp surfaces masked something more subversive. Upon reviewing *The Stuff* in 1985, *The Village Voice* hailed it as "something like Herbert Marcuse meets the Blob." Marcuse, the Frankfurt School philosopher of consumerist critique, alongside *The Blob*, a 1950s monster movie. This improbable pairing—highbrow social theory meeting unabashed B-movie nonsense— captures exactly the kind of hybrid genius that made Cohen's work so distinctive. Some years later, writing in the *New York Times*, Elvis Mitchell devoted an essay to "Larry Cohen's Art of Paranoia," praising how "Cohen's ideas have a B-picture power surge... at his best, he creates projects that center on stripping away skin, nerve endings, and, ultimately, pretense. Cohen can find entertainment in the belief that ignorance and insanity go hand in hand."

The mainstream press continued to catch on. *The New Yorker* did a profile of Cohen, and as *New York Magazine* put it in 2003, "Larry Cohen turned the grindhouses into arthouses, and the raincoat crowd didn't even mind," the article celebrating his "weird greatness" across a "long, weird career." Cohen himself embraced his B-movie tag, wearing it like a badge of honor. He once quipped that he was the John Cassavetes of exploitation cinema, which is less absurd than it sounds. If Cassavetes pioneered personal, independent filmmaking in the arthouse, Cohen brought the same renegade spirit to the grindhouse.

Q: The Winged Serpent.

In a 2025 essay for *The Quietus*, John Dornan characterized Cohen as "the Jonathan Swift of NYC," underscoring how firmly his reputation for savage social satire has endured within contemporary critical discourse. Cohen himself was always unapologetic about his eclecticism: "My pictures have a diversity to them… they're all bizarre ideas, but every one of them takes you to a different world." That spirit shaped both his methods and his movies. Cohen turned out high-concept romps with ideas bigger than their budgets, and his approach was simple: make the film "by any means necessary." If that meant shooting in the *New York Times* building (without permits), staging a gunfight at Grant's Tomb (without permits), or having Janine Turner pretend to pass out on a 5th avenue sidewalk while unsuspecting bystanders looked on (without permits), so be it. Chaos wasn't a problem—it was the point.

Cohen's final self-written, self-directed theatrical feature was *The Ambulance*, a mordant urban fantasy in which a mysterious emergency vehicle prowls New York, collecting patients it never delivers to hospitals. Eric Roberts plays a Marvel Comics artist, trading banter with Stan Lee in the

Colin Farrell and Larry Cohen on the set of *Phone Booth*.

artists' bullpen, where original comic art adorns the walls. Cohen commissioned Gene Colan to create a striking illustration for his unproduced screenplay *Headhunter*—artwork that can be glimpsed hanging in the bullpen scenes of *The Ambulance*.

Cohen recalled to *Sight and Sound* that his "first childhood hobby was drawing comic books," elaborate stories with "characters, surprise endings—quite adult in terms of content." That early fascination never left him. In the mid-1980s, he developed an unrealized *Doctor Strange* project for Marvel and Lee. *Headhunter* feels like the culmination of that lifelong obsession with comics, pulp invention, and urban paranoia. Its Phantom Physician is at once a costumed superhero and a quack doctor—a character springing from Cohen's comic-book imagination but refracted through the grit and volatility of New York street life.

Robin Wood argued that Cohen's work pivots on two recurring elements: the refusal of the "hero" and the motif of the double. *Headhunter* brings both to the surface. Kenneth Archer is no stable savior but a fractured figure, a failed doctor whose vigilante persona may "cure" criminals yet also embodies coercion and moral compromise, leaving audiences unsettled rather than reassured. His masked alter ego is simultaneously physician and executioner, healer and menace; the criminals he reprograms are distorted rather than redeemed, their violence redirected but not exactly erased. *Headhunter* thus dramatizes precisely what Wood identified as Cohen's bleak vision: society cannot repair itself, for its monsters are not aberrations but mirrors held up to its own anxieties. The Phantom Physician is such a hybrid creation—superhero and charlatan, outlaw and quack, comic-book fantasy refracted through the volatile materiality of New York street life.

The script's high-concept hook—a masked doctor who stalks the streets of New York at night, "curing" criminals with brain lasers—is outrageous yet instantly memorable. All of Cohen's signatures are present: New York seized as guerrilla backlot, pulp invention fused with urban paranoia, satirical flourishes that warp genre expectations. The set-pieces escalate with bravado, from courthouse gas attacks to "Phantambulance" chases and neon-lit explosions, spectacle no doubt straining against the limits of what would be Cohen's modest filming budget. Tonally, the script veers between comic-book camp, grotesque horror, and earnest melodrama. In Hollywood hands, such volatility might have been sanded into conventional smoothness; in Cohen's, it remains jagged, unpredictable, unmistakably his.

Larry Cohen passed away in 2019, leaving behind over a half-century of wild invention and razor- sharp wit. In his later years, Cohen found fresh financial success and belated Hollywood recognition. Yet as he joked to the *Los Angeles Times*, working as a writer-for-hire meant "sit[ting] down with producers, and producers are a real pain in the ass, believe me." When asked in *Screenwriter's Monthly* whether he would eventually regret not directing the hit *Phone Booth*

Photographs by Melissa Cohen.

himself, he answered, "I already regret it." Whenever possible, he preferred the chaos of independence, where he could do it his way—and only his way.

In his 77 (or perhaps 82) years—his disputed birthdate being perfectly in keeping with a life of tall tales—Cohen did it all: television and film, big screen and small, hits, flops, and everything in between. Repeatedly, he proved that significant ideas do not require significant budgets; with enough chutzpah, a filmmaker could smuggle biting social critique into the unlikeliest of genres, whether a creature feature about homicidal infants or a satire about sentient yogurt. He made the outrageous into the outrageously insightful, always in his own voice, always on his own terms. And so it is with *Headhunter*.

Because *Headhunter* was never produced, it remains uncorrupted: Larry Cohen's singular vision preserved on the page, undistorted. In that sense, it is still wholly his— bizarre, brilliant, and to use his own words, "individual and special."

SOME CALL HIM THE PHANTOM PHYSICIAN, OR THE MEDICAL MARVEL.

HE IS A MASKED VIGILANTE WHO NOT ONLY CAPTURES CRIMINALS BUT "CURES" THEM AS WELL.

THE POLICE CONSIDER HIM AN OUTLAW. MEDICAL SCIENCE BRANDS HIM A CHARLATAN.

BUT HE ALONE HAS DEVELOPED THE MIRACLE LASER BEAM THAT CAN RE-CHANNEL BRAIN WAVES AND MAKE PUBLIC ENEMIES INTO USEFUL CITIZENS AGAIN.

THE UNDERWORLD HAS GIVEN HIM A NAME:

HEADHUNTER.

PROLOGUE

EXT. WAREHOUSE DISTRICT, CENTRAL CITY,
USA—NIGHT

One of the old storage houses has been converted into a
smart discotheque—exclusive and far off the beaten path.
The block is lined with limousines, and huge bouncers block
the entry to the club. It is late and many upscale patrons
are leaving in small groups. These are sharply dressed guys
and gorgeous women, some happy, some quite stoned.
They search out their appropriate limos while others wait
impatiently for the valet to deliver their luxury cars.

One fashionable YOUNG COUPLE wanders around the
corner where they've found a parking place, only to discover
their BMW has a broken side window and the stereo system
has been ripped out.

The young man is furious. He shouts into the night at the
top of his lungs.

                    BOYFRIEND
          You bastards!!

All at once a half dozen figures materialize out of the
darkness: A STREET GANG in weathered leather outfits
and spiked haircuts. They surround the young couple,
threateningly.

                    GANG LEADER
          Did you call us?

                    2ND PUNK
          Got a further contribution to make to
          "the cause"?

                    GIRL
          Here—take my purse—just leave us alone.

The GANG LEADER grabs the purse and her wrist as well,
pulling her into an alley as the other gang members over

whelm her boyfriend. The gang leader shoves the girl into the arms of CHICO, the youngest of the gang members, a teenager who looks almost as scared as the victims.

> GANG LEADER
> Okay, Chico. She's all yours. Let's see you
> make your bones!

Chico strips off the girl's wristwatch and engagement ring, but he doesn't seem ready to do more.

> CHICO
> Look at this great Rolex. Let's go!

> GANG LEADER
> You're hurting the lady's feelings,
> rejecting her.

> 2ND PUNK
> Get it on, man.

Chico overcomes his reluctance, pulling the girl close and forcing a kiss. His fellow gang members shout their approval.

Then behind them a FIGURE steps into view, a shadow at first, quickly taking out the two gang members who have the boyfriend pinned against the wall. It all happens in a flash.

Two gang members suddenly lie doubled up on the pavement and A MASKED MAN IN A STREAMLINED SURGICAL GREEN COSTUME leaps into the midst of this human wolf pack. The gang responds instinctively with drawn switchblades, lengths of pipe and chain. The leader brandishes a .38 caliber revolver. The girl struggles to free herself from a thoroughly confused Chico.

> GANG LEADER
> Whoever you are, mister, you're dead
> meat!

                        HEADHUNTER
                Not mister. Call me "doctor."

                          CHICO
                What do you want?

                        HEADHUNTER
                Just your head. I'm going to turn it
                around.

The gang leader and his three remaining cohorts spring
forward, but Headhunter's reflexes are astonishing. He
avoids them and places a stiff karate kick below the largest
gang member's knee. It shatters and the youth collapses.

                        HEADHUNTER
                Your reflexes are perfect.

Another swift blow immobilizes Punk #2.

                        HEADHUNTER
                Tell me when it hurts.

He whirls, seizing the next young hoodlum by the crotch
and lifting him up off his feet.

                        HEADHUNTER
                Now cough!

The gang leader aims his .38 at Headhunter, who produces
an odd-looking gun of his own which fires a hypodermic
dart into his adversary's hand, paralyzing it so that he can't
pull the trigger.

                        HEADHUNTER
                You're into drugs, but I'll bet you haven't
                tried this one.

The gang leader staggers dizzily.

                        HEADHUNTER
                Pupils dilating. Blood pressure dropping.

The gang leader falls face forward on the ground, as stiff as a cardboard cutout.

Headhunter approaches Chico, who has backed into a corner holding an ice pick in his trembling hand.

> HEADHUNTER
> You're lucky. You haven't killed anybody
> yet, Chico. You can still be cured.

> CHICO
> You know me?

Headhunter gently plucks the ice pick out of Chico's hand and gives it to the young girl.

> HEADHUNTER
> (*to girl*)
> Call the police and have them picked up.
> (*pointing to Chico*) This one's mine.

He clobbers Chico with a swift uppercut. The young gang member collapses in Headhunter's arms.

> BOYFRIEND
> Where are you taking him?

Headhunter carries Chico off like a trophy of the hunt. In a moment he has vanished into the darkness of the night, leaving the young couple only a little the worse for wear, surrounded by the unconscious gang members, scattered in the alley like bowling pins.

In a moment a siren is heard close by, something similar to an ambulance siren but more high pitched and intense. It disappears into the distance and is gone.

We have met Headhunter face to face and seen him in action.

EXT. AERIAL SHOT—CENTRAL CITY—NIGHT

Flying low over the skyscrapers that make up this great metropolitan city. Over this we hear the siren but do not see the ambulance, which is speeding through this city carrying the phantom doctor and his newfound patient to the secret lair, which Headhunter calls his laboratory. Over this: MAIN TITLES ROLL.

FADE IN

INT. CRIMINAL COURTHOUSE, CENTRAL CITY—DAY

The steps of the courthouse covered with NEWSPAPER-MEN and REPRESENTATIVES of the media. Television cameras have been set up and cordons of POLICE hold back the SPECTATORS.

A POLICE VEHICLE pulls to the curb and DET. LT. SAM ROMERO emerges and passes through the police line. As he heads up the steps, newsmen call out to him.

                    NEWSMAN
                    (shouts)
        This must be a big day for you Lieutenant
        Romero.

                    PHOTOGRAPHER
        Look this way, please, Lieutenant!

But Romero continues up the steps paying no attention to the accolades. A uniformed police CAPTAIN greets him beneath the huge pillars that form the entry way to the great courthouse.

                    ROMERO
        How are we doing on security?

                    CAPTAIN
        Nobody gets inside without going
        through metal detectors. And we've got

armed guards at every entrance to the courtroom.

ROMERO
Your people have pictures of the woman?

The Captain reaches into his pocket and takes out a small reproduction of a photograph.

INSERT SHOT—THE PHOTO

A most beautiful woman. She could have been a top fashion model or even a film star, but there is a wildness in her, the "most wanted" woman in the United States.

ANGLE ON ROMERO AND THE POLICE CAPTAIN

Romero looks at the photograph with what is more than professional interest.

CAPTAIN
She's probably out of the country by now.

Romero looks around, scanning the crowd with his keen eyes.

ROMERO
I'll bet she's a lot closer than that.

Romero enters the building.

INT. CORRIDOR OF THE COURTHOUSE—DAY

A cordon of ARMED GUARDS escorts the prisoner to the court room in shackles.

The man's hands are cuffed behind him. His ankles are chained together so he can only take short steps. The prisoner is CARL LOMAX, perhaps the most dangerous man alive. Once a colonel in military intelligence, Lomax has turned on the country that honored and then disowned him, becoming the nation's most notorious outlaw.

The PROSECUTOR seems triumphant as he smiles over at Lomax.

Lomax is a strikingly handsome man with heavily chiseled features and coal black hair. But there is a fierceness about him that makes him frightening even in repose. Today he seems quite calm—not struggling against his shackles but rather waiting patiently and with a strange degree of confidence.

There are ARMED GUARDS at every entrance to the courtroom and spectators have not been permitted inside. Only token representatives of the press are there and they are now joined by Lt. Romero and other law enforcement officials who have come to hear the verdict of the jury.

No one pays particular attention to the mousy COURT STENOGRAPHER who now enters and begins setting up her stenographic equipment to transcribe the day's proceedings.

The BAILIFF calls the court to order.

                    BAILIFF
          The 32nd Circuit Criminal Court is
          now in session. Judge Harvey Morton
          presiding. Please rise.

JUDGE MORTON takes his place at the bench. The court stenographer begins pecking away on the small black box in front of her.

                    JUDGE
          Bring in the jury.

The court officers escort the JURY to their places. They look quite grim, most of them averting the glance of the defendant.

                    JUDGE
          Has the jury reached a verdict?

FOREMAN
We have, your honor.

JUDGE
Will you rise and read your verdict?

FOREMAN
We find the defendant guilty of eleven
counts of armed robbery.

A grin flashes across Lomax's face. He does not seem surprised. Instead, he looks back at Lt. Romero, raises both his shackled hands and waves.

LOMAX
Congratulations.

ANGLE ON ROMERO

Not amused.

ANGLE ON THE JUDGE

JUDGE
Colonel Lomax, you have disgraced the
trust this nation once put in you. You
broke the laws you had sworn to uphold
and have become a menace to every law-
abiding citizen...

WIDE ANGLE—THE COURTROOM

As Lomax addresses the Judge.

LOMAX
Your honor, may I speak?

JUDGE
The defendant will be permitted a brief
statement.

ANGLE ON THE JURY

Listening incredulously to this defiant man.

ANGLE ON LOMAX

> LOMAX
> Just like Ollie North, I broke the law—
> only in the interests of protecting the
> American people. The thanks I got was
> a twenty-year prison sentence which I
> had no intention of serving. Since then
> I've been an outlaw. You made me your
> enemy and you've learned to fear me.
> And I have plenty more lessons to teach.
> *(to the court stenographer)* Am I going
> too fast for you?

> STENOGRAPHER
> Slow down, will you? Who can keep up
> with this shit?

Abruptly the court stenographer stands up, lifting her stenographic box high over her head, and tosses it into the center of the courtroom.

The box EXPLODES and in an instant the courtroom is enveloped in a cloud of heavy gas.

The stenographer pulls a gas mask out of her briefcase, slipping it over her head quickly, then pulls out a second mask, tossing it to Lomax, who has already disposed of his two guards with two rapidly placed blows to the throat.

Although still chained, Lomax slips the mask over his head with ease while the other occupants of the court are gasping for breath and collapsing.

Romero runs down the aisle toward the defendant reaching for his gun. He has it out and is pointing it but he can't see where to fire. He's surrounded by blinding fumes. Other police officials are stumbling into him and collapsing.

ANGLE ON THE JURY

as they are overcome and pass out.

ANGLE ON THE JUDGE

asleep behind the bench.

ANGLE ON THE COURT STENOGRAPHER

as she removes her wig to reveal a head of long, cascading, blonde hair, that we recognize as belonging to ILONA, the beautiful woman in the photograph.

ANGLE ON LOMAX

as he searches the pockets of the guards for keys that will unlock his shackles. He finds them and quickly frees himself, collecting the guns from the unconscious guards and tossing one to Ilona.

                    ILONA
          We need a hostage.

                    LOMAX
          Grab Romero!

ANGLE ON ROMERO

On his knees, crawling along the floor, struggling to remain conscious. He looks up as Ilona kicks the gun out of his hand and drags him to his feet. She's quite strong and able to lift his entire weight. She tosses him across her shoulder like a sack of potatoes and carries him up the aisle, preceded by Lomax armed with a gun in each hand.

INT. CORRIDOR, COURTHOUSE—DAY

Lomax and Ilona emerge with their solitary hostage. Ilona has her revolver pressed up against Romero's head, ready to pull the trigger if her demands are not immediately met.

ILONA
Everyone up against the wall or the
Lieutenant gets it first!

The police have no choice but to comply.

CAPTAIN
They've got Romero. Do as they say.

ILONA
Faces to the wall. No peeking.

She and Lomax hurry down the corridor with their hostage
in tow. No one makes any attempt to stop them.

CUT TO:

EXT. BASEBALL STADIUM, CENTRAL CITY—DAY

A game is in progress, now in its sixth inning. The bases are
loaded. The crowd CHEERS as the new BATTER takes his
place at the plate.

ANGLE ON THE STANDS OF SPECTATORS

One of whom has a portable radio in his lap and has just
heard a special news bulletin. He stands up and shouts to
everyone around him:

SPECTATOR
Hey, it just came over the radio. Lomax's
girlfriend Ilona busted him out!

2ND SPECTATOR
Shit. I don't believe it.

Like wildfire the word spreads throughout the crowd.
CAMERA PANS as people are on their feet everywhere,
shaking their heads in disbelief. Others laughing. Some even
cheering the escape.

ANGLE ON A BOX BEHIND HOME PLATE

Some of the best seats in the house currently occupied by KENNETH ARCHER, a good-looking young executive type in his late twenties. His companions, ROBERT and JIM are both yuppies, successful enough to take an afternoon off from work at their own discretion.

> JIM
> That's the kind of woman I'd like to have on my side.

> ROBERT
> Yeah, sure. As if you could handle her.

> KEN
> Not exactly my type.

> BOB
> I guess you'd throw her out of bed, huh?

> KEN
> I guess if she wanted to make love to me I wouldn't have much choice, would I?

CUT TO:

INT. KEN ARCHER'S HOME—DAY

A custom-built private home in a suburb close by the city. A place cluttered with toys and gadgets, almost as if a kid lived there instead of an adult.

Ken returns home after the ball game. He goes to a desk and unlocks the bottom drawer with a key. He takes out a scrapbook and sits behind the desk, flipping on the lamp. Slowly he turns the pages as CAMERA MOVES in closer over his shoulder. We see that there are newspaper clippings and magazine articles, all carefully pasted into the album. And each of them has to do with the elusive female public enemy, Ilona. Her face is as familiar to the public as that of a film star, and yet no one has been able to capture her.

One headline reads: "THOUSAND DOLLAR A DAY NEW YORK MODEL TURNS TO CRIME."

A cover story from *Playboy* says: "THE MOST BEAUTIFUL CRIMINAL ALIVE," with a color photo spread of early fashion photos of Ilona before she embarked on her life as an outlaw.

A *People* magazine cover shows Ilona and her partner Lomax in a pose reminiscent of Bonnie and Clyde. Certainly these two have become the subject of much media hype. A page clipped out of the *Inquirer* reads: "Fugitives Ilona and Lomax, Will They Wed?"

ANGLE ON KEN ARCHER'S FACE

He turns page after page. It's evident that he's obsessed. What he failed to admit to his friends is that he thinks constantly of this young woman who cannot be tamed.

The telephone RINGS. Ken answers it.

                    KEN
        Yes?

An authoritarian VOICE is heard on the other end of the line.

                    VOICE
        I thought to remind you about the family
        dinner Friday night at seven. And try not
        to do anything to embarrass me this time.

                    KEN
        Yes, sir.

The phone clicks off and Ken hangs up. Picking up a weekly news magazine he begins to tear out yet another article about Ilona. In doing so he catches his finger on one of the staples that holds the magazine together. He stares at the tiny drop of blood on that finger. He seems oddly transfixed, almost frozen. The sight of blood does something to him.

Ken gets up and crosses to a floor-to-ceiling mirror on the far wall. He stares at himself in the mirror as one might stare at a stranger. Then he exerts pressure on the left side of the mirror and it springs open—like a door—revealing a passageway beyond.

Ken steps through, closing the mirror-door after him.

CUT TO:

INT. THE HIJACKED POLICE VAN—NIGHT

Ilona is at the wheel. Lomax behind her seated next to their prisoner, Det. Lt. Romero who is neatly trussed up with his hands cuffed behind his back.

                    ROMERO
          How long are you going to keep hauling
          me around town? Kill me and get it over
          with!

                    LOMAX
          That's not up to me. You belong to Ilona
          now.

                    ILONA
               (to Lomax)
          You didn't tell me he was so attractive.

                    LOMAX
          I think she's trying to make me jealous.

                    ILONA
          Do you like me, Lieutenant Romero? Do
          you think we could ever get it on?

                    ROMERO
          Not if you were the last woman I ever
          slept with.

                    ILONA
          That can be arranged.

                                LOMAX
            I've got another present for you.

He reaches into his pocket and produces a jewel encrusted
ring with a huge purple stone in the center which he slips
on her finger.

                                LOMAX
            Bought if off a guard in the lockup.
            Claimed he took it away from a high-
            priced hooker.

                                ILONA
            I've never seen a stone that color before.

                                LOMAX
            Maybe I was robbed.

Ilona leans over and plants a grateful and lingering kiss on
Lomax's lips.

                                ROMERO
            Don't mind me.

EXT. THE POLICE VAN—NIGHT

As it pulls into a parking lot behind a two-story building
which bears a sign: "CENTRAL CITY HEALTH SPA—
OPENING SOON."

Ilona and Lomax haul their captive out of the van. Ilona
dutifully slings the trussed up detective over her shoulder
like a sack of laundry.

                                ILONA
            A woman's work is never done.

She uses a key to unlock the service door of the gym and
proceeds to tote Romero inside, while Lomax returns to the
van.

> LOMAX
> He's all yours, sweetie. Have fun.

Lomax pulls away, leaving the lieutenant to Ilona's tender mercies.

CUT TO:

INT. POLICE HEADQUARTERS—NIGHT

Chief of Police HOGAN confers with key law enforcement OFFICIALS.

> HOGAN
> They just located the getaway van, floating in the South River and Lt. Romero wasn't in it.

> POLICE CAPTAIN
> I'd hate to be in his shoes.

CUT TO:

INT. GYM—NIGHT

EXTREME CLOSE UP—ROMERO

as he's being kissed passionately on the mouth by the gorgeous Ilona.

CAMERA PULLS back to reveal that Romero is securely tied by his wrists and ankles to a huge exercise machine, an apparatus King Kong might well have worked out on. Ilona breaks the kiss and steps back. They are in a large mirrored exercise room in the new hi-tech gym.

> ILONA
> That was just to get your circulation going.

Now she switches on the exercise machine and the involuntary workout begins. In a few seconds, Romero is huffing and puffing but can't free himself from the apparatus.

ILONA
You'll be in great shape before you die.

ROMERO
You're not scaring me, Ilona. I know
you never killed anybody. That's your
boyfriend's department.

ILONA
That's only because my aim is good. I've
wounded a lot of very important people.

ROMERO
I can't figure you out. You had everything
before Lomax came along.

ILONA
Everything but Lomax. *(she laughs)* Sure,
I could've made more modeling than
stealing, but I was bored. That face on
the magazine covers was all makeup and
lighting. This is the real me!

She turns up the controls on the machine. Romero is forced
to exercise still faster.

Then, without warning, the door leading to the steam
room opens behind her and clouds of steam drift into the
gymnasium. Ilona turns in time to see the SILHOUETTE
of a FIGURE in green surgical costume and mask step into
view.

Romero is likewise surprised at the unexpected entrance
of the notorious figure known only as HEADHUNTER.
He wears a circular reflector disc on his forehead which
seems to emit spasms of light. It has an immediate hypnotic
quality—an ability to slow reflexes.

Ilona herself seems totally disoriented by the appearance of
this bizarre-looking physician.

                    ILONA
            What are you? What do you want?

                  HEADHUNTER
            To change your mind.

Ilona points her gun directly at him, but a sudden blast of
light from the reflector disc momentarily blinds her.

                  HEADHUNTER
            It'll take several minutes for your optic
            nerve to recover.

Ilona fires her gun. The bullet misses by inches.

                    ILONA
            I can still hear you!

                  HEADHUNTER
            Can you?

All at once the small square VOICE BOX he wears around
his neck causes an ECHO and his words resound off all the
walls, bouncing back and forth. He seems to be in a half
dozen places at once. "Can you, can you, can you???"

Ilona seems frightened for the first time. She doesn't know
which direction to turn.

ANGLE ON LT. SAM ROMERO

still exercising against his will.

                   ROMERO
            Lay off her, Headhunter. She's mine.

                  HEADHUNTER
            All you could do is lock her up.

                   ROMERO
            You've got no right to do this.

ILONA
What is he talking about?

ROMERO
The sonofabitch wants to operate on you.

ILONA
Nobody's going to cut me!

She fires another shot that goes wild.

HEADHUNTER
It's a non-invasive procedure. There'll be
no scars.

ROMERO
(coaching her)
Ilona—aim to your left. More left! Aim
low. Get him in the leg!

Ilona follows instructions and indeed her gun is pointed
directly at Headhunter. But he somersaults forward kicking
the gun out of her hand just as it goes off. He takes hold of
her wrist and she tries to struggle free.

ILONA
How did you find me here?

HEADHUNTER
As long as you're wearing that ring, I'll
always know where you are. I designed it
myself.

ILONA
You planted a goddamn homing device on
Lomax. You bastard.

She swings at Headhunter, who counters with a short
upper cut to the tip of her jaw. Ilona collapses into his arms.
Headhunter flips off the exercise machine on which Romero
is imprisoned.

HEADHUNTER
Now, wouldn't you have felt awful if
she'd shot me?

ROMERO
Come on, Headhunter. Leave her. I need
the arrest.

HEADHUNTER
She'll never break the law again. You have
my word on that.

ROMERO
What good is your word? A quack with a
mask on—practicing medicine without a
license!

Headhunter ignores the criticism. He scoops Ilona up in his
arms and carries her out.

CUT TO:

EXT. FRONT ENTRANCE, THE GYM—NIGHT

Headhunter's phantom ambulance is parked in the shadows,
a long sleek ambulance in the style of the 1940s customized
to suit Headhunter's purposes.

As Headhunter approaches with Ilona, the rear door slides
up into the roof and a large transparent cylinder extends.

Headhunter opens the tube and gently places Ilona inside.

TIGHT ON ILONA. Her sight and her consciousness
returning. She looks up at that masked face—into those
eyes.

ILONA
Where are you taking me?

HEADHUNTER
My hospital.

The tube closes, and Ilona is instantly overcome by an anesthetic gas within. She sleeps peacefully now. The tube withdraws into the "Phantambulance" as Headhunter gets behind the wheel and pulls off into the night. In an instant he is gone.

CUT TO:

INT. HEADHUNTER'S LABORATORY—NIGHT

Compact, but with advanced equipment far beyond what might be available in any other hospital on earth. This is a laser laboratory of the highest sophistication. The laser gun that Headhunter aims at Ilona's forehead radiates immense energy to pinpoints of the brain and has the power to permanently alter the flow of brain waves.

MONTAGE SEQUENCE.

Headhunter works meticulously through the night, constantly cross checking with a bank of computers which provide three-dimensional replications of the patient's brain on a projection TV screen.

Ilona lies on a chrome surgical table, motionless, as the hours pass. And the thin laser beam continues to do its work.

MULTIPLE SHOTS—COMPUTER LIGHT SHOW (WHAT'S GOING ON INSIDE OF ILONA'S HEAD)

A barrage of bizarre images. We see her as a top runway model in Paris and as a cover girl, then as a bank robber in the midst of a heist—the two conflicting sides of this woman's personality.

In the laser induced fantasy, we see Ilona blown away by the bank's security guards, shot to pieces by a barrage of automatic weapons. Then her quite dead, bullet-scarred body is back on the runway modeling again, her high-fashion gown stained with blood.

INT. HEADHUNTER'S SURGICAL CHAMBER—
DAY

Headhunter wheels Ilona to a recovery area and anxiously awaits her return to consciousness.

> ILONA
> What happened to me?

> HEADHUNTER
> Lie back. Don't try to get up. I'll dim the lights.

> ILONA
> Nothing hurts.

> HEADHUNTER
> All your vital signs are excellent. You'll be on your feet in a few days.

> ILONA
> I feel so—different.

> HEADHUNTER
> You are different.

> ILONA
> I—died. It was so real... yet I couldn't die. I was up there parading around doing turns.

> HEADHUNTER
> What else?

> ILONA
> I remember... I tried to hurt you, didn't I?

> HEADHUNTER
> You could never do that again.

ILONA

Did you use some drug on me?

HEADHUNTER

No drugs. No medication. Your brain
waves have been altered, re-channeled.

ILONA

How?

HEADHUNTER

A gadget I invented. Spent most of my
life savings building it, and, surprisingly,
it works.

ILONA

What'll happen to me now?

HEADHUNTER

What do you want to happen?

ILONA

I don't know! I just want to stay here...
with you.

HEADHUNTER

When you're strong and you've got your
confidence back, we'll give you a new
name. A chance to start over.

ILONA

Why do you do this? What's in it for you?

HEADHUNTER

What's in it for any doctor? You were
sick, now you're going to get better.

ILONA

Where is everybody else? Do you do this
alone?

HEADHUNTER
It all works off a central computer.

ILONA
Even the Lone Ranger had Tonto. *(beat)*
Don't you ever take off your mask?

HEADHUNTER
Never in front of a patient.

ILONA
Then you still don't trust me. You're not
sure I'm cured.

HEADHUNTER
You can prove that to me.

ILONA
How?

HEADHUNTER
By assisting in Lomax's capture, before he
does any more harm.

ILONA
Lomax…

HEADHUNTER
He was a great soldier, an American
hero—once.

ILONA
I was in love with him—

STEEL
But not anymore?

ILONA
All of a sudden I can't imagine how I ever
let him get close to me.

> HEADHUNTER
> That's all over. Let it go. No guilt, no
> anger—just look straight ahead toward
> what's going to be. *Your new life.*

> ILONA
> Don't you want to use your laser machine
> on Lomax too?

> HEADHUNTER
> It's too late for him. I don't treat killers.
> We'll let the police have him.

Headhunter prepares to leave the recovery room.

> ILONA
> You're not going to leave me here alone?

> HEADHUNTER
> I promise I'll be here when you need me.
> Now close your eyes and rest.

He exits. Ilona lies back dreaming, a smile on her lips. She seems totally content.

CUT TO:

INT. ARCHER MANSION—NIGHT

The weekly dinner party is in progress. Friends and family of DR. CLEMENT ARCHER in dinner jackets and evening gowns represent the upper crust of the city. Ken Archer is present along with his sister, DR. MARGARET ARCHER. MAYOR FENTON KEESLEY is the guest of honor, along with JONATHAN HOGAN, the frazzled Chief of Police.

> KEESLEY
> As chairman of the State Medical
> Association, what's your opinion of this
> Headhunter fellow?

CLEMENT

A complete charlatan. It's one thing
experimenting on convicts in prisons
when they volunteer, but this fellow's
kidnapping his patients.

MARGARET

He claims he can make useful citizens out
of them again.

HOGAN

But they never pay for their crimes! What
about the victims? What about justice?

KEN

I thought the whole purpose of the
system was to rehabilitate?

KEESLEY

You're not a doctor, are you, young man?

KEN

Absolutely not. My father's the surgeon
and my sister's the psychiatrist. I'm the
black sheep.

MARGARET

My clever little brother invented the hula
hoop or the Frisbee! Or was it the slinky?

KEN

Close. I created a few toys that caught on.
Novelties. Like this one.

Ken takes a small object out of his pocket and bounces it
on the table. It's a hexagon-shaped ball that hops across
the table jumping dinner plates and dodging crystal wine
glasses, never colliding with anything, and finally bouncing
back into Ken's hand.

KEN

It avoids contact with obstacles and it
always comes back.

HOGAN

What the hell do you call that?

KEN

The Hex. And every kid is going to want
one.

MARGARET

I have no idea what he does with all his
money.

CLEMENT

Kenneth could have been a fine physician
if he'd put his mind to it.

KEN

I hate to contradict my father in front of
company, but I flunked out of first year
medical school. Couldn't stand the sight
of blood.

CLEMENT

You'd have learned to *love* the sight of
blood. We all have. He did it just to upset
me. Simply to get attention.

MARGARET

I've heard of marching to a different
drummer, but Ken has his own brass
band.

KEN

I'm lucky I still get invited to these
dinners.

MARGARET

You usually end up as the principal subject
so you have to be here to defend yourself.

KEN

I thought Headhunter was the subject
tonight. Now, he's what I call a genuine
eccentric.

MARGARET

Sociopath is the word.

CLEMENT

If I may make a suggestion, the best way
to capture the bastard is to turn the public
against him.

HOGAN

He can't be cruising around this city
without being spotted by somebody, That
phantom ambulance doesn't exactly blend
in with the scenery. If we had the public
on our side...

KEESLEY

That's an excellent solution, Dr. Archer.
The medical association will denounce him
in the press and on television as a phony.

HOGAN

We'll have a 24-hour switchboard set up
to receive information, and post a hefty
reward.

CLEMENT

Now, shall we adjourn to the study for
some coffee and a cigar?

KEN

Well, I don't smoke and coffee makes me
nervous.

He crosses and hugs his father. Dr. Clement Archer returns
his son's embrace. He really cares for the young man, it's
just that he's been such a major disappointment.

CLEMENT
Try not to invent anything silly this week
if possible.

KEN
Father doesn't view me as a very serious
person. (*Ken crosses and shakes hands
with the mayor.*) Good night, Mayor
Keesley. I wish I'd voted for you. I forgot
to register.

KEESLEY
I assumed as much.

KEN
(*turns to Hogan*)
I'd like to call you up if I may during the
week, I have a few dozen parking tickets
you might be able to help me with.

CLEMENT
Stop trying to influence public officials in
my home!

KEN
Sorry. (*kissing Margaret on the cheek*)
Good night, doc.

MARGARET
Good night, Kenneth. Drive carefully.
Stop at red lights.

KEN
Don't worry. Tonight I'm walking.

The BUTLER brings Ken Archer his overcoat and he
departs from the dinner party.

EXT. MANSION—NIGHT

Ken comes through the gate to a quiet residential street lined with gated homes. He begins walking casually, lost in his own thoughts.

DISSOLVE TO:

EXT. ANOTHER SECTION OF TOWN—NIGHT

Ken still strolling along. Then, as he passes an office building, he hears a MOAN coming from behind a steel gate in an alley. He pauses and hears it again. Ken tries the gate and finds it unlocked. CAMERA FOLLOWS him into the alley where he finds the body of a UNIFORMED SECURITY GUARD lying on the ground. Ken leans over the man who has been struck over the head and is bleeding.

GUARD
Thank God you found me. He's up there.

Ken looks up, in the direction the injured guard is pointing.

KEN'S POV—THE SIDE OF THE BUILDING

A cat burglar, a HUMAN FLY, is scaling the wall.

BACK TO KEN AND THE GUARD

GUARD
He must be headed for the Gemstone
Company on the fourteenth floor. You
got plenty of time. Get help!

KEN
You're bleeding...

GUARD
I'll be okay. What are you staring at? Why
don't you go get help?

Ken rises to his feet but seems dizzy and disassociated. The sight of blood has caused him to blank out and, *when he recovers, he isn't the same person anymore.* His voice and his demeanor are different. His very identity has altered.

                    GUARD
        What happened to you?

                    KEN
        I'm fine now. I've got to go home and get
        something. It's just around the corner. I'll
        be right back!

Ken hurries out of the alley, moving with speed and energy.

ANGLE ON WALL OF THE BUILDING ABOVE

as the acrobatic crook grabs onto a cornice, swinging back and forth until he gains his foothold.

On his belt he wears a grappling hook connected to coils of wires, which he now tosses up.

TIGHT SHOT

The grappling hook catches on the ledge above.

ANGLE ON THE CLIMBER

Using the wire, he's able to surmount the gargoyles that protrude as obstacles in his path.

Once above the gargoyles, he reaches the fourteenth floor window which has always been his destination.

TIGHT SHOT—THAT WINDOW

as the Human Fly jimmies the window open and slides inside.

INT. GEMSTONE COMPANY OFFICES—NIGHT

The lights have all been extinguished. Only the moonlight slips through the windows. The Human Fly makes his way across the showroom, past the empty display cases in the direction of the vault. He strips off his gloves to reveal long sinewy hands, the fingers surprisingly sensitive, like a concert pianist yet unbelievably strong.

DISSOLVE TO:

SOME TIME LATER

THE HUMAN FLY—STILL AT WORK

He finally unlocks the safe and opens it to reveal a CACHE OF PRECIOUS GEMS. The Human Fly grins in triumph. Then he hears a sound that disturbs him. He turns in time to see an odd locking HEXAGON-SHAPED BALL bouncing across the hardwood floor in his direction. We've seen such a ball before. The Hex! Ken Archer's newest contraption. The ball bounces around the amazed thief in full circle, then completes its journey by bouncing back into the hand of Headhunter! A powerful figure in a green medical uniform with a surgical mask hiding his identity.

CLOSE-UP—THE HUMAN FLY

Surprised and stunned by the sudden appearance of Headhunter, he goes for his gun but the phantom physician is too quick for him, twisting the weapon out of his grasp then thrashing his acrobatic opponent despite the Human Fly's agile efforts to defend himself. It's a splendid display of martial arts combat but the Human Fly is no match for the Medical Marvel.

HEADHUNTER
You require a strong anesthetic!

Headhunter knocks him cold, then drags him off by his feet.

EXT. ALLEY BEHIND BUILDING—NIGHT

The Phantambulance is again parked here. Its rear door slides upward silently by remote control. The cylinder extends to receive the new patient. Automatically, the Human Fly is placed in a condition of temporary hibernation. Now the doors of the Phantambulance slide closed again.

ANGLE ON HEADHUNTER

taking his place behind the wheel.

HIGH ANGLE SHOT

as the Phantambulance springs to life, like a shadow sweeping through the city streets. No sign of life can be seen through the glass, which is completely coated.

The bullet-like black ambulance picks up tremendous speed and soon vanishes into the night.

CUT TO:

INT. HEADHUNTER'S SURGICAL CHAMBER—NIGHT

The Human Fly now dressed as a patient lies in the path of the massive laser gun which even now is aimed at his fore head and is forever altering his brain waves and his destiny.

Headhunter supervises the procedure still masked.

In a glass observation booth behind him, Ilona watches. A mesmerized spectator.

ANGLE ON THE SURGICAL TABLE

Headhunter removes the laser momentarily and swings another object into place suspended on a gantry above the surgical table. It looks very much like a camera only with two lenses. He switches it on. The lenses are projectors aimed at the face of the patient. Headhunter flips a switch automatically from the remote control panel he holds in his hand.

The projection begins. CAMERA MOVES in on the patient. We can see the projection across his face as if it is the screen where the drama is being played out.

All at once, the Human Fly's eyes open wide. The light is projected into his pupils. The images seem to sharpen to focus indirectly on his eyes. CAMERA MOVES IN on those eyes.

WE SEE WHAT HE SEES. THE IMAGE IS THAT OF THINGS FALLING. THE CAMERA DIVES HEADLONG INTO THE GRAND CANYON, PLUMMETING DOWN TOWARD THE ROCKY FLOOR BELOW.

CUT TO:

ANOTHER IMAGE OF FALLING

CAMERA IS PLUNGING DOWN FROM A SKYSCRAPER INTO THE BUSY STREETS OF THE CITY WHICH BEGINS TO SPIN, CREATING A TERRIFIC SENSE OF VERTIGO. JUST AS THE CAMERA REACHES THE SIDEWALK, THE IMAGES SEEM TO FRAGMENT—TO BREAK UP—TO SHATTER.

AS IF TO GIVE THE EXPERIENCE OF STRIKING THE PAVEMENT WITH TREMENDOUS FORCE.

CLOSE-UP—HUMAN FLY

as he begins to SCREAM. He's experiencing this.

Formerly a man who feared no heights, he's now being taught the terrors of falling. It is being programmed into his mind, etched into his psyche.

ANGLE ON HEADHUNTER

as he shuts off the apparatus. A glass bubble descends over the patient who now sleeps.

Only then does Headhunter realize that he's not alone in the chamber. Ilona has come down the steps from the observation booth.

                    HEADHUNTER
You shouldn't be down here.

                    ILONA
You made him afraid.

                    HEADHUNTER
He'll never climb again.

                    ILONA
He must have been very brave... before.

                    HEADHUNTER
He only looked up. I made him
look down. He'll find himself a new
occupation on the ground. Something
honest.

                    ILONA
Is it fair what you did to him?

                    HEADHUNTER
Would it be more fair locking him in a
crowded cell for twenty years like an
animal?

                    ILONA
I don't know. Can you come upstairs
now?

                    HEADHUNTER
In a little while.

                    ILONA
I've fixed you a wonderful dinner with
whatever I could find in that kitchen of
yours.

HEADHUNTER

Why don't you go and look after it. I'll
try not to be too late.

ILONA

You won't ruin my dinner?

HEADHUNTER

I need to be here when he recovers.

ILONA

Couldn't you just keep him asleep until
after the meal is over? I mean, I've been
working all day to make this special.

HEADHUNTER

You've made every evening special.

ILONA

I just want to please you.

HEADHUNTER

And you do.

She throws her arms around him.

ILONA

I want to please you more! I can't kiss
you with that silly mask on. Why must
you wear it? There's no one here but us.

HEADHUNTER

Let's just say I feel safer with it on.

Without warning, she pulls off the mask. Revealing Ken's
face.

ILONA

How could anyone be comfortable hiding
such a beautiful face?

HEADHUNTER
Now you've got to forget what you've seen.

ILONA
Not yet.

She leans forward and kisses him softly on the lips. He immediately responds. The kiss becomes more passionate.

HEADHUNTER
We'd better stop. *(kiss)* This isn't ethical. *(kiss)* I'm your doctor.

Then he forgets his moral objections and just enjoys it.

DISSOLVE TO:

INT. ILONA'S CUBICLE ADJACENT TO THE LAB

Headhunter and Ilona are naked in bed together, lost in passionate lovemaking. For Ken it is the fulfillment of a fantasy. He has bedded the girl of his dreams.

Ilona is totally wild and remarkably athletic under the sheets and Ken surprises himself by satisfying her again and again. She's a skillful and inexhaustible partner. But it's more than sex. She seems to totally adore him.

MULTIPLE DISSOLVES:

THE BED

As the lovemaking goes on deep into the night until finally Ilona rolls over and falls into a slumber with a complacent smile on her beautiful face. Ken looks down at her.

HEADHUNTER
Well, at least you haven't forgotten any of that.

DISSOLVE TO:

INT. ILONA'S CUBICLE

Ken is up and getting dressed, slipping back into the costume of "Headhunter" once again. Ilona awakens and sees him putting on the gear and the mask.

                    ILONA
        You're not getting tired of me already?

                    HEADHUNTER
        Tired of you? Never.

She reaches down and kisses his hands, or his gloves, which he has just slipped into.

                    ILONA
        You're always so covered up.

                    HEADHUNTER
        The patient is waking up. He needs me.

                    ILONA
        I'm sorry. I was being selfish again.

She runs onto the stairs, heading halfway up to the observation booth. She wraps herself in a sheet and follows him down the spiral stairs to the surgical chamber. CAMERA FOLLOWS them below to the laboratory.

                    ILONA
        I'll learn! I really will try!

He's ignoring her, raising the transparent dome up from above where the Human Fly is recovering. His attention is on his patient now, but Ilona just won't go away.

                    ILONA
        When you see me being selfish, call it to
        my attention. That'll be helpful. Darling?
        (beat)

                    HEADHUNTER
          I heard you.

CLOSE-UP—ILONA

Now her feelings are hurt again. She pouts, then finally exits
back upstairs.

ANGLE ON HEADHUNTER

He hears the door finally close and breathes a sigh of relief.
She's gone at last. He leans over his patient.

                    HEADHUNTER
          How do you feel?

                    HUMAN FLY
          Feel. I keep getting killed—over and over.
          I'll never want to climb again.

                    HEADHUNTER
          And you'll never take anything that
          doesn't belong to you.

                    HUMAN FLY
          Where the hell am I?

                    HEADHUNTER
          Think of it as a delivery room. You've just
          been reborn. You can try to get up now.

The Human Fly looks over the edge of the surgical table.
He's only five feet off the floor, but already he has got a
dizzy spell.

                    HEADHUNTER
          What's the matter?

                    HUMAN FLY
          Shit. I could fall.

                    HEADHUNTER
          I'll help you down.

The Human Fly lowers himself carefully to his feet, abnormally afraid of even the slightest height.

> HEADHUNTER
> You'll be more comfortable on the ground.

CUT TO:

INT. DINING ROOM, HEADHUNTER'S PRIVATE QUARTERS—NIGHT

Ilona has set for the evening feast. The table is virtually laden with food. Candles are burning, the lights are dimmed, Montovani's hokey music is flooding the room with its syrupy themes. The salad has been tossed, the wine has been poured, and yet poor Ilona is alone at the table. Headhunter has not yet arrived.

She might have expected as much.

She looks at her feast, the work she's gone to, and she feels very sorry for herself. She downs a glass of wine, then pours herself still another.

> ILONA
> Well, I'll eat by myself!

DISSOLVE TO:

INT. HEADHUNTER'S BEDROOM—NIGHT

A spartan room down the corridor from the lab. Ilona sits in the bed voluptuously dressed only in a towel with what's left of the last of the bottle of wine beside her in the bed. It looks like she's been crying all evening.

Her dinner has been ruined and she's still waiting for Headhunter, who has yet to show up.

Finally the door opens, a shadow falls across the bed. She turns eagerly, then a look of disappointment crosses her face.

WIDER SHOT

Headhunter is there all right, but still in costume, still masked.

> ILONA
> I ate my dinner alone… and then I ate
> your dinner too… and most of the wine.

> HEADHUNTER
> I wasn't hungry.

> ILONA
> Why do you still have that damned
> costume on?

> HEADHUNTER
> A tip just came in from one of my
> informants. There's a shipload of illegal
> armaments coming into Pier 12 tonight…
> in about forty minutes. The munitions
> dealer must be a very sick man.

> ILONA
> *(jumps out of bed)*
> Don't you think I'm beautiful anymore?

> HEADHUNTER
> The most beautiful woman in the world.

He kisses her quickly — without much interest.

> ILONA
> It was so much better without that mask.

In a moment Headhunter is gone. The very lovely and frustrated young woman stares at her gorgeous figure in the mirror, turning in circles, searching for some sign that she's putting on weight. She's obsessed by the thought.

> ILONA
> It's only been five days, and look at me!

EXT. STORAGE WAREHOUSE—NIGHT

The Phantambulance pulls out of the secret garage and sweeps off into the city on to another journey.

EXT. PIER 12—NIGHT

A freighter is moored at the pier and a bale of cargo is being lowered from the hold onto the dock. Then the cable seems to SNAP—and the entire shipment falls, splitting the wooden crates wide open and revealing the contents. HIGH POWERED AUTOMATIC WEAPONS. AN ARSENAL!

The group of ARMS SMUGGLERS panic and rush to scoop up their property when they find themselves confronted by the stranger in the mask and costume. Headhunter himself.

                    HEADHUNTER
        Looks like I busted your toys, gentlemen.

The arms smugglers are desperate men and they themselves are armed to the teeth with M-16s and automatic pistols. They open fire instantly, but flashes from Headhunter's reflective disc headgear blinds them and makes them easy prey. Their shots go wild. Headhunter wades into them, slamming a few heads together. Headhunter uses the torn cargo net which held the shipment to tie up and incapacitate the whole mob. Then he approaches the HONCHO of the mob.

                    HEADHUNTER
        Next patient, please.

                    GUN RUNNER
        This shipment is worth millions. I can
        make you rich.

                    HEADHUNTER
        And I can make you better. This'll only
        hurt for a second.

He uses his trusty hypodermic gun to render his new patient unconscious. He turns to the others who are securely trussed up.

> HEADHUNTER
> I'll try to send some federal agents around
> before gangrene sets in.

And he carts off his new patient who is already sleeping as peacefully as a baby, while the other gunrunners struggle futilely with their bonds.

CUT TO:

INT. ILONA'S BEDROOM — NIGHT

She's propped up on the bed munching gourmet cookies which she dips into an open pint container of Häagen-Dazs Vanilla Swiss Almond. Ilona is pigging out and watching television.

ANGLE ON TV SCREEN

ABC's "Newswatch." The TV host Ted Koppel is interviewing medical experts, most prominently Dr. Clement Archer (Ken's father).

> KOPPEL
> So you see this Headhunter as a definite
> threat to the well-being of the American
> public?

> CLEMENT
> This man is circumventing the nation's
> legal system, performing these horrendous
> operations. In my opinion, he's a dangerous
> sociopath. The worst criminal of them all.

ANGLE ON ILONA

She's stopped eating. My God, she's lost her appetite.

TIGHTER SHOT ON TV SCREEN

                    CLEMENT
        It's the duty of every decent citizen to
        help us catch this man.

                    ILONA
        "Decent." That's me now!

She uses the remote control to switch off the television set.
She can't bear to hear anymore.

She crosses to her closet and takes out one of the new outfits
that Headhunter has bought for her. She tears off the tags
and starts to get dressed.

                                    DISSOLVE TO:

MED. SHOT—ILONA, getting dressed. She has gained
so much weight she can barely zip herself into the dress.
She struggles, holding her breath, she finally succeeds, but
she feels like she's bursting out of her clothing. She looks at
herself in the mirror in despair.

                    ILONA
        Nothing fits! What is this guy doing to
        me?

                                    DISSOLVE TO:

INT. THE LAB—MORNING

Ilona slipping quietly down the spiral staircase, passing
Headhunter's private research laboratory. She peers through
the glass partition.

HER POV

Headhunter in his mask and uniform working feverishly
over the gun runner he's captured.

He doesn't look up. He doesn't realize that Ilona is leaving
the premises.

INT. GARAGE BELOW—DAY

Ilona reaches the foot of the stairs, moving past the Phantambulance, which is parked in the darkness.

She locates the exit which leads to the street and unbolts it, slipping quietly outside.

EXT. DOWNTOWN STREET, CENTRAL CITY—DAY

Ilona is surprised to find herself amid the hustle and bustle of the downtown metropolitan area. This is the first time she's been outside since her capture by Headhunter.

The SOUNDS of the city crowd in around Ilona. The pounding of the power drivers, the rumble of the huge vehicles. All this mixed in with the cacophony of the passing taxis and the traffic jam at the main intersection nearby. Through all this she hears the voice of Dr. Clement as he spoke on television.

> CLEMENT'S VOICE
> "A dangerous sociopath... the worst criminal of them all. Help us catch this man!"

CAMERA MOVES IN TIGHT ON ILONA. She knows what she must do.

HER POV—DIRECTLY AHEAD

The steps leading up to the entrance to the main Police Headquarters.

CUT TO:

INT. LT. ROMERO'S OFFICE—DAY

It's lunchtime. The squad room is quiet. Only TWO MEN on duty in a far corner questioning a WITNESS as Ilona comes up the stairs and crosses to the cubicle which bears Romero's name.

ANGLE WIDENS

to reveal Romero at his desk typing up a report. He looks
up and is startled to find himself in the presence of a woman
who recently held him captive.

Romero comes to his feet, reaches for his shoulder holster,
pulling out his snub-nosed service revolver and pointing it
unsteadily at Ilona. He's obviously scared of her.

> ROMERO
> Stay right where you are!

> ILONA
> Lieutenant Romero?

Ilona continues crossing the cubicle approaching him. She
doesn't have any weapon. She's not even carrying a handbag.
But Romero remembers what she did to him last time and
he's not going to let her get any closer. She approaches. He
begins to back away around his desk, even though he's got
the gun.

> ROMERO
> *(shouts)*
> Hey, somebody get in here. Officer,
> I need assistance.

Romero stumbles over his chair, almost falls. Ilona reaches
out to steady him. Romero pulls away.

> ILONA
> Why are you so afraid of me?

> ROMERO
> You don't remember nearly pulling my
> arms out by the roots??

> ILONA
> Now that you mention it. But why did I
> do that?

ROMERO

For fun.

ILONA

I only came here to help you. I know all
about Headhunter.

ROMERO

Now I get it. Trying to trade your own
freedom in exchange. It won't wash.

At that moment two other DETECTIVES rush into the
cubicle.

OFFICER

Are you all right?

ROMERO

It's okay. I'm fine now.

OFFICER

Who's she?

ROMERO

An informant, that's all. You can leave us
alone.

OFFICER

A moment ago you were yelling for
assistance.

ROMERO

I made a mistake. I thought she was
somebody else.

The two detectives leave. Romero holsters his firearm.

ROMERO

Sit down.

ILONA

I feel like I'm walking through somebody
else's dream.

ROMERO

Did Headhunter work on you?

ILONA

How did you know?

ROMERO

I've seen that same stoned expression
before. What about Lomax? Do you
remember Lomax?

ILONA

I'm sure I do.

ROMERO

This man.

He takes a "wanted" circular out of his desk.

ILONA

He's great looking.

ROMERO

Yeah. And that isn't even a good picture
of him.

ILONA

Can I keep this?

ROMERO

It's all coming back to you, isn't it?
You were with Lomax for three years.
Together you stole close to ten million
dollars.

ILONA

That wasn't very nice of us.

ROMERO

He's still at large. But Headhunter nabbed
you and "changed you."

ILONA

Yes, I am different. I've gotten ugly and
lazy and I sleep all the time...and eat. He
never pays any attention to me.

ROMERO

Can you take us to him?

ILONA

It's my duty, isn't it?

ROMERO

Duty? Oh sure. And the judge and jury
will take that into account.

ILONA

I love him so much, but they say he's a
threat to society.

ROMERO

Where'd you hear that?

ILONA

Ted Koppel said so.

ROMERO

Then it's got to be true. Where is this
laboratory of his?

ILONA

It's not far. I can show you.

ROMERO

You wouldn't be trying to walk me into
another trap?

ILONA

I must have been a terrible person for you
to think that.

And she begins to cry, burying her face in Romero's
shoulder.

ROMERO

Now take it easy. You're not supposed to
cry. Ilona would never cry.

ILONA

Oh, I must look awful.

ROMERO

A little puffy maybe but still lovely.

ILONA

I wish *he'd* said nice things like that to
me.

ROMERO

He's not capable of loving anybody. He's
an egomaniac.

ILONA

He got inside my brain. He made me love
him. But he never cared about me. I won't
be sorry when you arrest him, Lieutenant.
I won't be sorry at all.

CUT TO:

EXT. STORAGE WAREHOUSE—DAY

A dozen police cars pull up from all directions and ARMED
OFFICERS emerge carrying riot guns, tear gas equipment,
and assault weapons. This is a massive raid by the Central
City Police Department on Headhunter's secret lair.

ANGLE ON POLICE VEHICLE

as Romero and Ilona climb out of the back seat. Chief Hogan is with them.

>   HOGAN
>   You better be telling us the truth, young
>   lady.

>   ROMERO
>   She is.

>   POLICE SERGEANT
>   All the doors are sealed. How do we get
>   in?

>   ILONA
>   I don't know.

>   ROMERO
>   We'll have to blast our way in.

>   HOGAN
>   Cordon off the street and bring in the
>   demolition team.

ANGLE ON DEMOLITION TEAM

as they approach the garage doors with their explosive devices. They have just reached the doors when they shatter and the Phantambulance plows through at top speed. Its siren is a deafening SCREAM scientifically designed to incapacitate all those in the immediate area.

ANGLE ON HOGAN

as he holds his ears and falls to his knees. CAMERA PANNING to the other police who are attempting to take aim and fire at the Phantambulance but instead clasp their hands over their ears trying to shut out the shrill shriek of the super vehicle.

ANGLE ON ILONA

as she screams, also clutching her ears.

HER POV as the Phantambulance comes straight at her. HIGH ANGLE SHOT as the Phantambulance zigzags between the parked police vehicles, knocking one of them out of the way, then another, like pins in a bowling alley.

Police officers attempt to fire but their aim is diverted by the intense pain. They can barely keep their eyes open, much less fire at a moving target.

A few bullets do strike the Phantambulance but bounce off since it is armor-plated.

> POLICE SERGEANT
> (*shouts*)
> Shit! It's bulletproof! Go for the tires.

The police make a futile effort to disable the vehicle but many of them have already fallen to the sidewalk with their arms wrapped around their ears trying to make the pain subside.

ANGLE ON THE PHANTAMBULANCE

as it careens toward a construction site at the end of the street, crashing through the wooden fence.

EXT. CONSTRUCTION SITE—DAY

as the Phantambulance plows straight ahead, construction workers dodging in all directions, ladders toppling leaving workers dangling above the ground. The ambulance races to the other side of the construction site, decimating the opposite fence and disappearing off into the distance leaving behind several dozen confused HARD HAT WORKERS scattered on the ground trying to recover, their ears still ringing.

ANGLE ON THE FRONT OF THE WAREHOUSE

The police stagger to their feet, their ears pounding. Chief Hogan shouts commands but nobody seems to be able to understand him.

> HOGAN
> Radio on ahead. Set up roadblocks. He's headed east...

> POLICE SERGEANT
> What?

> HOGAN
> How do I know what I said? I can't hear myself think!

> ILONA
> You let him get away.

> ROMERO
> Talk into this ear. His laboratory is up there, isn't it? At least we've got that.

Romero strides forward, waving to the other officers.

> ROMERO
> Follow me.

INT. HEADHUNTER'S SECRET LABORATORY — DAY

as the police burst in, followed by Chief Hogan, Romero and Ilona.

> HOGAN
> Look at this. It must have cost millions to build. (*to the cops*) Well, you know what to do.

The police officers armed with hatchets and clubs begin to demolish the laboratory, smashing everything. The giant computer sizzles and explodes, glass shatters, the laser guns short circuit in a 4th of July burst of energy.

ROMERO

Look out!

The cops run for their lives as a chain reaction occurs. One unit after another detonates as the cops take cover. Romero pulls Ilona to safety.

The pyrotechnics display continues with Headhunter's precious apparatus detonating into a flash of fire and sparks.

Then all at once there is utter silence. The laboratory is a sea of smoldering ashes.

POLICE SERGEANT

Well, it's done.

POLICE CAPTAIN

Maybe we should have left something for the scientists to look at.

HOGAN

And let it fall into someone else's hands? No, it's better destroyed.

ROMERO

At least we put a stop to these crackpot experiments.

HOGAN

How do we know she didn't warn Headhunter in advance? He was ready for us!

ILONA

Headhunter changed me. And that's why I had to do this to him. Because now I know the difference between right and wrong.

HOGAN

Lock her up. And I want extra security on her twenty-four hours a day.

Hogan departs. Romero and Ilona stand looking at the smoldering laboratory, the wreckage of a man's dream.

CUT TO:

EXT. SOUTH RIVER BRIDGE—DAY

The Phantambulance crashes through police barricades and a barrage of gunfire to head across the bridge.

Police vehicles are in immediate pursuit.

VARIOUS SHOTS—THE CHASE

Beneath the elevated train tracks—zigzagging in and out between immense steel pillars. The ambulance maneuvers spectacularly. Police cars crash into the pillars, others go up on the sidewalk through store windows.

And above it all, the SHRILL SCREAM of the siren a decibel so high that the windshields of the police cars shatter in the faces of the drivers and they lose control of their vehicles.

ANGLE ON PHANTAMBULANCE

The high-pitched shriek of the super siren causing store windows to crack sending a spray of glass from one end of the block to the other.

ANGLE INSIDE LOCAL APARTMENT

An average FAMILY watching television. The beer bottle on the table in front of them EXPLODES, then the television screen, and then their windows as well.

INT. LOCAL BAR—NIGHT

As again the siren is heard. Coming still closer, the hundreds of liquor bottles behind the bar shatter as do all the glasses held by customers. But people are too busy holding their ears to even notice the calamity.

An IRISHMAN at the bar begins to shout:

IRISHMAN
It's the cry of the banshee!!!

CUT TO:

EXT. NEON SIGNS ABOVE THE BARS AND
RESTAURANTS—NIGHT

as they too begin to quiver and then explode as the Phantambulance passes by zigzagging in and out of traffic.

ANGLE ON DRIVERS

as they pull to the curb and hold their ears—leaving a path
through which Headhunter's vehicle can easily maneuver.

ANGLE ON HEADHUNTER

at the wheel, driving with the carefree skill of an Indianapolis
speed racer. Then up ahead he sees—

HIS POV

A WOMAN and a CHILD in a carriage frozen in the center
of the street. He's headed right for them.

ANGLE ON HEADHUNTER

as he swerves.

ANGLE ON THE PHANTAMBULANCE

as it crashes through a steel fence into a small pocket park
which is mostly deserted at this hour of night except for a
few sleeping VAGRANTS.

The scream of the siren sends the vagrants running for their
lives. The ambulance takes out several benches, the monkey
bars and two sets of swings before coming to rest in the
huge sandbox.

ANGLE ON HEADHUNTER

Thrown forward by the impact, he bangs his head on the steering wheel, cutting a small gash above his eye. It begins to bleed. A second later he recovers.

The siren of the Phantambulance is droning away, losing its power. But it is replaced by other sounds, that of police sirens coming ever closer.

EXT. THE WRECKED PHANTAMBULANCE— NIGHT

As Headhunter opens the door and clambers out. He's still unsteady but he hears the sirens coming and knows he has no time to waste.

He runs forward vaulting the far fence of the small park and running down the narrow streets.

Lights are going on in the apartment buildings that surround him, but the streets are deserted. Headhunter rounds A JUNKYARD.

A mongrel DOG chained to the fence barks at him viciously but Headhunter takes no notice of the animal. He seems totally disoriented.

TIGHTER SHOT

as Headhunter raises his hand to his forehead and feels the dampness. He looks at his fingers. They're covered with blood.

TIGHT SHOT TO HEADHUNTER'S EYES

He's startled by the sight of the blood on his fingertips. For it is blood that triggers off the switch in his multiple personalities.

The dog keeps barking furiously. Headhunter backs further into the junkyard tripping over old items like tricycles, spare tires and twisted heaps of metal.

There is battered furniture and finally a giant mirror with a crack running through it.

It is in front of this mirror that Headhunter pauses and stares at himself.

There is no longer a Headhunter. He is Kenneth Archer. He draws closer to the mirror and looks intently at himself, then down at the costume he wears.

                    KEN
          Why am I dressed like this?

He pulls off the mask and stares at his face, and at the gash on his forehead. He feels quite sick.

And suddenly the NIGHT WATCHMAN is upon him. A burly old man with a broken nose who's used to dealing with vandals at this time of night. He's surprised to see a grown man in a surgical uniform.

                    WATCHMAN
          Well, what are you done up for?

                    KEN
     I don't know.

                    WATCHMAN
          You're trespassing. Better get a move on.

                    KEN
     What is this place?

                    WATCHMAN
          You're about a mile from South River
          Bridge.

                    KEN
          These clothes… (*beat*) Have you got any
          regular clothes?

                    WATCHMAN
Just some junk in the pile over there. Take
anything you want for a dollar.

                    KEN
I don't think I have any money.

                    WATCHMAN
Then make it an even trade. Leave what
you're wearing, but get on with it. A man
has got to get some sleep.

                    KEN
Thanks.

He quickly moves toward the shack outside of which stacks
of old clothing are piled in mounds. He searches through,
trying to find something wearable.

                                    DISSOLVE TO:

ANGLE ON KEN

Changing out of the costume. Somehow he's glad to be rid
of it. He looks at the uniform one last time as if it represents
something fearsome to him, something unknown. Then
he rolls it up and tosses it into the pile with the other old
clothes. He's found a pair of slacks, a t-shirt and a somewhat
threadbare jacket that just about fit.

As he walks away and the CAMERA MOVES around the
stack of clothing, we see that he has left behind his utility
belt, his weapons, all his articles of defense. He is now
only Ken Archer, an ordinary man with an extraordinary
dilemma, a man who cannot remember what he's been
doing for the last 48 hours.

EXT. NEARBY STREETS—NIGHT

ANGLE ON KEN

stumbling along the sidewalk. A crowd has clustered around the crashed police cars and the broken windows, and around the park where the Phantambulance is now being searched by uniformed cops. Police barricades have been put up.

Onlookers are being herded back.

Ken Archer is merely one of the crowd. The blood on his forehead has been wiped away. There's only a slight gash now and the bleeding has stopped. He looks like another of the bewildered residents who have come downstairs from their apartments to see what broke their windows and nearly shattered their eardrums.

ANGLE ON KEN

as he looks at the wreckage of the custom-built ambulance curiously as he's never seen it before, then continues walking.

EXT. SOUTH RIVER BRIDGE—NIGHT

Ken heads back across the bridge, an isolated figure moving toward the lights of the city, the magnificent Central City skyline.

CUT TO:

EXT. SMALL FASHIONABLE TOWNHOUSE, EAST SIDE OF THE CITY

NIGHT

Ken approaches and rings the doorbell. When no one replies he leans on the buzzer insistently. Finally a maid's voice is heard on the other side of the door.

MAID

Who is it at this hour?

KEN

Kenneth Archer. I need to see my sister.

The door opens and the maid notices the cut on his forehead.

MAID

Been in an accident or something?

Ken brushes by her and enters.

INT. FIRST FLOOR OF THE BROWNSTONE—
NIGHT

Margaret is halfway down the stairs just tying her bathrobe.
She hurries to her brother.

MARGARET

What happened to you?

KEN

I'm not sure. What is today?

MARGARET

It's Sunday, first thing in the morning.
What's the matter with you?

KEN

I don't remember anything since Friday
night.

MARGARET

Have you had these blackouts before?

KEN

Yes, plenty of times, but I always woke
up in my bed. But tonight I…

MARGARET

(to maid)

That's all right, Edna, you go back to sleep.

MAID

You sure you don't want a pot of coffee?

MARGARET

That would be a good idea.

She leads her brother into her ground floor office and turns on the lights.

INT. MEDICAL OFFICE—NIGHT

The office boasts a separate entrance for patients.

MARGARET

Let me put something on that cut.

KEN

It doesn't hurt.

MARGARET

How did it happen?

KEN

I don't know. I woke up wandering in a junkyard across the river, and when I looked at myself I was wearing some kind of surgical costume. And a mask.

MARGARET

It was a dream.

KEN

Maggie, it was real. I know the difference.

MARGARET

We'll have plenty of time to talk about it in the morning.

KEN

No, there isn't time. Maggie, I'm two people, maybe more.

MARGARET
I knew you were eccentric, always putting
on costumes even as a kid.

KEN
It's not funny, Maggie. I need your help as
a doctor.

MARGARET
I shouldn't be treating you. I'm
personally involved.

KEN
It must be the sight of blood that does it.
That's what triggers the change.

MARGARET
That same reaction made you drop out of
Pre-med in the very first week.

KEN
And I disappeared that time, didn't I? For
almost two weeks.

MARGARET
We all thought you took off because you
didn't want to face dad.

KEN
I couldn't remember where I was that
time either. Maggie, it's happened to me
off and on for years.

MARGARET
Tell me what you want me to do.

KEN
You've put patients under hypnosis before.

MARGARET
I think what you're suggesting could be
very dangerous.

                              KEN
            It's more dangerous not knowing who I
            am.

                         MARGARET
            Sit down and roll up your sleeve.

                              KEN
            Pentothal?

                         MARGARET
            Look, I'm the doctor. All you have to do
            is relax and answer questions.

She crosses to her cabinet and removes a fresh hypodermic,
inserts a new needle and opens a drawer containing various
vials of liquid. She selects one and fills the hypo with its
contents.

Margaret giving Kenneth the hypo.

Kenneth falling into a deep slumber.

                                        DISSOLVE TO:

Margaret seated opposite him, waiting, looking at her watch,
reluctant to go through with it but seeing no alternative.

                                        DISSOLVE TO:

THE SLEEPING CITY—NIGHT

Millions of citizens are asleep and dreaming, but no dream
as fantastic as Ken Archer's strange odyssey.

                                        DISSOLVE TO:

INT. PRISON CELL—NIGHT

Ilona pacing her cell. She cannot sleep. She has betrayed
Headhunter—caused his laboratory to be destroyed. And
now she wonders whether she did the right thing.

DISSOLVE TO:

CLOSE-UP—KENNETH ARCHER

Still deeper in his slumber.

ANGLE WIDENS

as Margaret seats herself beside him, turns on a tape recorder and begins to speak softly.

> MARGARET
> We're going back now, Ken. As far back
> as you can remember. We're kids riding
> our bikes. You just got your new Schwinn
> and we're on a country road together. Do
> you remember that?

> KEN
> Yes.

> MARGARET
> You weren't looking where you were
> going and you ran into a ditch and fell.

> KEN
> Yes. It bent the whole bike out of shape.
> Dad was furious. My first time riding it.

> MARGARET
> And you cut your knee. Very badly.
> I tried to stop the bleeding and you
> laughed and said it didn't hurt.

> KEN
> It didn't. I guess I was more worried
> about what dad was going to say.

> MARGARET
> So we lied about what happened.

KEN

We made up a story that some driver ran
me off the road.

MARGARET

But the sight of blood didn't bother you
then. You joked about it. How old were
you?

KEN

I was eight.

MARGARET

Then something happened after that.
When was the next time you saw blood?

KEN

I don't remember.

MARGARET

Yes, you do. Was it the following year
when I was off at school?

KEN

I was lonesome after you were gone.

MARGARET

Yes, we were so close. Then when I
came back it was never the same. What
happened that summer?

KEN

I can't think.

MARGARET

Mother went away. Does that have
anything to do with it?

KEN

No... I mean, I don't remember.

MARGARET

You do remember. *(beat)* I was happy
to be out of the house. They never got
along anymore. He'd be gone for days at
a time. You must have heard all that. The
arguing—the accusations.

KEN

It woke me up... the yelling.

MARGARET

Yes?

AS KEN RELATES THE STORY WE BEGIN TO SEE
IT UNFOLD ON THE LEFT SIDE OF THE SCREEN
JUST AS HE DESCRIBES IT. (AND WE NOTE THAT
IN HIS MEMORY HIS MOTHER BEARS A STRIKING
RESEMBLANCE TO ILONA. THEY ARE BOTH
TALL, EXOTIC TYPES.)

KEN

I knew I wasn't supposed to come
downstairs. They were in his study. She
said she was going to go away... from
him... from all of us. That she never
wanted to see any of us again.

MARGARET

There's more, Ken. What else?

KEN

I ran down the stairs. I was going to say,
please don't go, but before I got to the
door, he hit her. She fell up against the
desk and when she turned around she had
this... I don't want to talk anymore.

MARGARET

Tell me what you saw.

KEN

She had this small silver-plated gun. It looked like a toy. And then when he came toward her again it went off and he screamed and fell down. I ran in and knelt down—and touched him.

MARGARET

He was bleeding.

KEN

His shirt was soaked with blood. Then I looked up at her... and she wasn't even sorry. For a minute I thought she was going to shoot me too. Then she put the gun back in her handbag and went out. I heard the car drive away. By then, dad was on his feet again tending to his own wound. But there was blood all over my hands. Then I don't remember anything else. I think I passed out.

MARGARET

Dad never reported the shooting to the police. Nobody else ever knew except you.

KEN

I asked him once. He said it had been a dream. That it never happened. (*beat*) Just like you tried to tell me about tonight.

MARGARET

It happened all right. I'm going to count to ten now and you can wake up and you'll remember *everything* that we've spoken about.

She begins to count. CAMERA PULLS AWAY from them, brother and sister reunited again after all these years. Their estrangement has been set aside. The mystery of their past suddenly unlocked.

KEN
Margaret. I remember.

She puts her arms around him and hugs him tight.

MARGARET
I love you, Ken. I'm sorry it took me so
long to say so.

And he hugs her back.

CUT TO:

EXT. THE OLD POLICE HEADQUARTERS
BUILDING—DAY

An antiquated four-story structure built in the late 1950s.
A huge water tower stands on the roof. CAMERA MOVES
in on the upper floor. The windows here are all barred. This
is the location of the detention cell block where criminals
are held during interrogation.

INT. CELL BOCK—DAY

CAMERA MOVING TOWARD an isolation cell at the far
end of the corridor. It is here that particularly dangerous
felons are kept—away from the other prisoners. Lt. Romero
is just emerging from this cell, in which Ilona is incarcerated.

ROMERO
You'd better see a lawyer before you sign
any confession.

ILONA
I want to sign it. I did all those things—
and more!

ROMERO
You're going to be quite a witness against
Lomax when we nail him.

ILONA

I know how you can do that.

ROMERO

I'm open to suggestions.

ILONA

Just surround this place and wait.

ROMERO

You think he'd risk everything to rescue
you?

ILONA

You said I broke him out of the
courthouse. Now it's his turn. He's very
loyal, I think.

ROMERO

Well, I've already thought of that. We've
got sharpshooters in the windows of the
adjoining buildings and undercover cops
all over the streets.

He signals the guard to lock the steel security door which
runs from floor to ceiling.

ROMERO

And we're keeping you locked up in this
maximum security area. He'll never get
near you.

ILONA

You don't know him very well.

CUT TO:

MONTAGE—DAY

WINDOWS OF BUILDINGS AND HOTELS
SURROUNDING THE POLICE HEADQUARTERS.

70

Snipers are at their posts, ever watchful for an appearance by Lomax.

THE STREETS NEARBY

A hot dog vendor, homeless derelicts, maintenance men repairing the sidewalk. They are all undercover cops, heavily armed. The trap has been set. But where is the quarry?

ANGLE ON SNIPER IN HOTEL WINDOW

watching through telescopic sight.

CAMERA RISES from that window to the ROOF three stories above. A metallic tube protrudes over the parapet of the roof. It moves further into position and we realize this is the muzzle of a powerful mortar.

The sudden BLAST of the mortar seems to make the building tremble.

EXT. POLICE HEADQUARTERS—DAY

as the mortar shell hits its target: the ancient water tower. It is an explosive shell that blasts the tower to splinters and sends tons of water crashing through the roof of the police station.

REACTION SHOT—THE SNIPERS

as they watch the roof collapse under the impact.

INT. THE CELL BLOCK BELOW—DAY

as it is instantly flooded with water. The prisoners in their cells are in danger of drowning like rats!

                    CHIEF GUARD
          Open the cells. Get them out before they
          drown!

The cells are automatically opened. The prisoners swim out—the water is already rising over their heads. But Ilona is still trapped in that isolation cell with an airtight floor to ceiling steel door that will keep the water out.

The guards are also trying to keep afloat. Among them, Lt. Romero alone seems to be struggling to get back into the flooded cell block rather than out of it.

> ROMERO
> Ilona is still in there. Where's the key?

> CHIEF GUARD
> Save yourself!

> ROMERO
> Give me the key.

> CHIEF GUARD
> The floor can't handle the weight of this
> flood. It's going to cave in any minute —

The Chief Guard surrenders the key to Romero, who swims past the escaping prisoners in the direction of Ilona's cell. The electric lights are flickering out. The cell block is plunged into darkness.

Romero is forced to swim underwater to find the keyhole and unlock the steel door. As he opens it, water rushes into the cell pinning Ilona to the concrete wall. Romero swims to her, wraps an arm around her, and together they paddle out.

The water has nearly reached the ceiling in the corridor.

> ROMERO
> Hold your breath!

Romero and Ilona struggle underwater, making their way up the submerged corridor.

EXT. POLICE STATION—DAY

as fire trucks pull up and emergency personnel rush inside, all uniformed in firemen's gear.

INT. MAIN FLOOR, POLICE STATION—DAY

Water is knee high and is running down the staircase from above in torrents. The firemen minister to the officers and prisoners who have suffered injuries during the flooding of the cell block upstairs.

Romero appears on the staircase supporting Ilona, who is both soaked and dazed. A fireman rushes to the foot of the stairs to assist them.

Then we recognize the fireman as LOMAX.

Romero realizes it's Lomax just an instant before he is hit across the throat by a carefully aimed karate chop. Romero crumbles and Lomax grabs him, gently lowering him to the floor as if he's one of the many injured.

Then Lomax scoops Ilona up and rushes outside with her as if she's a casualty, elbowing past more firemen who are still entering.

EXT. THE POLICE STATION—DAY

Lomax carries Ilona to the closest fire truck, quickly slugging the driver and pulling him out of the cab of the vehicle.

Two other fire fighters attempt to intervene. Ilona does nothing to assist Lomax as he disables both his adversaries. He looks over at Ilona who seems totally disassociated with what's going on.

                    LOMAX
        Well, don't do anything to help out.

ILONA

Please don't hit them again.

LOMAX

Get in the truck!

Ilona climbs into the passenger seat of the fire truck. Lomax takes the wheel.

WIDER SHOT

The police snipers open fire on the truck as Lomax guns the engine, knocking parked police cars out of the way and clearing a path up the street.

Lomax and Ilona escape in the huge fire truck, while the undercover cops on the sidewalk riddle the vehicle with bullets.

But in a moment the fire truck has vanished around the corner.

DISSOLVE TO:

EXT. CENTRAL CITY HARBOR, NOT FAR FROM THE FERRY TERMINAL—DAY

A battered tugboat is moored out at the end of the old pier. In the distance the large commuter ferry wearily carries passengers and cars back and forth across the bay.

CAMERA MOVES in on the seemingly unoccupied tugboat.

INT. CABIN, TUGBOAT—DAY

This is the new hiding place for Lomax and the recently rescued Ilona. He's heating coffee on a hot plate.

LOMAX

Change into some dry clothes while I fix
you up a hot breakfast.

ILONA

Thank you.

LOMAX

You knew I wouldn't leave you there.

He pulls her close and tries to kiss her on the mouth. She turns her head away.

LOMAX

What's wrong with you?

He looks her over from head to toe as if to be sure this is really the same girl.

LOMAX

How could you let that retard, Romero,
capture you?

ILONA

He didn't. It was Headhunter.

LOMAX

There is such a guy?

ILONA

Not anymore. The police raided his lab.
They destroyed everything.

LOMAX

How would you know?

ILONA

I led them there.

LOMAX

So you made a deal with the D.A.?

ILONA

No. No deal.

LOMAX

How'd you ditch Headhunter in the first
place?

ILONA

He trusted me. He thought I was in love
with him.

LOMAX

I won't ask any questions. Whatever you
had to do, you had to do. All that matters
is I've got you back.

He takes her in his arms and kisses her. She allows it but
puts no passion into her response. He pushes her away.

LOMAX

Jesus! What did that bastard do to you?

ILONA

You just said you weren't going to ask.

LOMAX

It was worse than getting into your pants.
He got into your head!

ILONA

He made me realize how wrong we are,
Lomax.

LOMAX

Shit, you were perfect before he got his
hands on you. Perfectly rotten! I hope
the cops find him and blow his pious ass
away.

ILONA

Lomax, you're in love with somebody
that doesn't exist anymore.

LOMAX

He ruined you.

ILONA

I'm so confused. Even when I turned him
in, I thought: "He'll be proud of me for
doing this." Now that doesn't make any
sense, does it?

LOMAX

I think I'll sleep up on deck tonight.

ILONA

Don't you want to be with me?

LOMAX

I'm not like your "medical boyfriend." I
don't take advantage. When you decide
you want me, I'll be there.

Indeed Lomax is a most honorable villain. He wants Ilona
back but only on his own terms. She must love him again
first.

CUT TO:

MONTAGE SEQUENCE—MULTIPLE ARRESTS!

as Headhunter's former patients are finally apprehended by
the authorities.

INT. FLOWER SHOP—DAY

as the police rush in and arrest a timid FLORIST, formerly
a womanizing criminal at large.

POLICE SERGEANT
All right, O'Connor, you're under arrest
for armed robbery!

O'CONNOR
How did you find me?

POLICE SERGEANT
I guess Headhunter shouldn't have kept
such complete files on his patients. Put
the cuffs on him.

A uniformed POLICEWOMAN approaches O'Connor.

O'CONNOR
No! Don't let her touch me. Keep her
away from me, please. (*breathlessly*) You
do it. Not her.

POLICE SERGEANT
What's the matter, O'Connor? Afraid
of girls? I thought you only victimized
women! Cuff him.

O'Connor breaks down in tears as the policewoman roughly
handcuffs him. He recoils from her touch. He's been cured
all right. He now has a phobia about women.

CUT TO:

INT. SWANKY RESTAURANT—DAY

as the MAITRE D' is taken into custody by still another
POLICEMAN. He's the former Human Fly whom we saw
Headhunter take into custody and "rehabilitate."

HUMAN FLY
Where are you taking me?

DETECTIVE
We're extraditing you back to Central
City. Take him to the airport.

HUMAN FLY
No airplanes. I'm getting sick just
thinking about it.

DETECTIVE
How about that? All of a sudden he can't
stand heights. Somebody really did a job
on you.

HUMAN FLY
Yes, he did. That goddamn Headhunter.
He ought to have his license taken away.

DETECTIVE
What license?

And they remove the Maitre d' from the restaurant as the
patrons look on in confusion.

CUT TO:

INT. TAXICAB—DAY

A PASSENGER gets in. We recognize the cab driver as
Chico, the young gang member Headhunter "reformed."

CHICO
Where to?

DETECTIVE
Police Headquarters. You're under arrest,
Chico.

CHICO
I've been living a good clean life. I work a
twelve-hour shift, don't bother nobody.

DETECTIVE
You forgot to throw the meter.

CHICO
I ain't the same person no more.

DETECTIVE
Where have I heard that before? Oh yeah,
it was in Headhunter's files.

CHICO
He turned me in?

DETECTIVE
More or less. Can't you go any faster?

CHICO
I don't exceed the speed limit. That would
be breaking the law.

DETECTIVE
Well, we wouldn't want you to do that.

CUT TO:

NEWSPAPER HEADLINE: *"CURED" FELONS
RECAPTURED, PATIENTS OF HEADHUNTER TO
STAND TRIAL*

INT. OFFICES OF THE ARCHER TOY COMPANY—
DAY

Ken Archer sits behind his desk which is covered with
contraptions that he has concocted out of his fertile
imagination. The walls are lined with reproductions of
advertisements for the products that Archer has created, all
useless novelty items from a Pet Rock to a Slinky, things
that have become a part of our culture and made millions
for him, but nothing that would be considered useful to our
society.

Ken is reading the newspaper which recounts the recapture
of the very people he sought to reform through his medical
technology. His SECRETARY brings in his lunch on a tray.

KEN
Sorry, Betty, not hungry today.

BETTY
Maybe you should see a doctor.

KEN

I've had enough of doctors for the rest of
my life. And enough of toys.

BETTY

What's the matter?

KEN

All of a sudden I feel like I've wasted my
life. Look at all this junk.

BETTY

People seem to like it. At least they buy it.

KEN

They use it for five minutes and then
never look at it again.

BETTY

By the way, there's been a detective up
here for the past couple of hours asking
everybody questions, and now he says
he'd like to see you.

KEN

Is his name Romero?

BETTY

As a matter of fact, it is.

KEN

All right, send the man in.

Ken crosses and looks at himself in the mirror. Does he bear
any resemblance to the elusive Headhunter? Will Romero
recognize him? He turns as Romero enters the office.

ROMERO

Mister Archer.

KEN

Please have a seat.

Romero sits down and then jumps up as an obnoxious sound is emitted from the chair.

> KEN
> I'm sorry. That's just one of our Whoopee cushions. It's kind of a running joke around here.

Romero removes the Whoopee cushion from the chair and tosses it aside.

> ROMERO
> You seem to have a lot of fun at work. Your employees seem to like you.

> KEN
> That's nice to know. How can I help you, lieutenant?

> ROMERO
> You've probably heard of Headhunter.

> KEN
> Is there really such a person?

> ROMERO
> Oh, yes. Behind that mask is a very brilliant man. Even a genius.

> KEN
> I don't think I've ever met any geniuses.

> ROMERO
> We destroyed his laboratory, and now we're trying to trace the medical equipment and the computer elements that went into it. He must have spent millions.

> KEN
> We only manufacture toys here.

ROMERO

Yes, but a number of foreign suppliers
traced their invoices to your company.
You paid the bills for a criminal
enterprise.

KEN

Did I? Then somebody's taking
advantage of me. That's probably why
my employees like me so much. I'm a
pushover.

ROMERO

We'd like your permission to take full
inventory of your books. Maybe we can
find out who diverted these materials to
their own use.

KEN

Sure. By all means.

Ken crosses from behind his desk and shakes hands.

KEN

I'd like you to take home some samples of
our products for your kids.

ROMERO

I'm not married.

KEN

Or in love?

ROMERO

Do I look like a man who's in love? (*beat*)
As a matter of fact, I am. Unfortunately,
when I catch her again, she's going away
for twenty years to life.

KEN

I guess that could be called an
occupational hazard, lieutenant.

He walks Romero to the door.

                    ROMERO
          It must take a remarkable mind to think
          up crazy stuff like this.

                    KEN
          And get somebody to buy it!

Romero leaves. For the moment Ken is alone and safe.

                    KEN
                 (to himself)
          You'll never catch him, Romero. He's
          gone—forever.

                                        CUT TO:

INT. INTERROGATION ROOM—DAY

Romero and the FBI men question a number of the criminals
Headhunter managed to rehabilitate and who now have
been re-arrested.

                    ROMERO
          Help us find Headhunter and the D.A.
          will show his appreciation.

                    SPEED
          After what he did to me, he should burn!
          I was the best getaway driver in the
          business. And now I go into a cold sweat
          trying to parallel park.

                    GUN RUNNER
          He got me so I'm afraid of guns!

                    CHICO
          He ruined our lives!

DRUG DEALER
Actually, my health food store was doing
great. And I've never looked better.

FBI MAN
Get them out of here!

DRUG DEALER
You ought to try these niacin tablets for
your nerves.

FBI MAN
What's he doing with pills? Don't you
search the prisoners in this jail?

ROMERO
Let me have a couple of those pills. I can
use them.

CUT TO:

INT. CENTRAL CITY INTERSTATE BANK—DAY

TV cameras monitor the day's transactions. A solitary
BANK GUARD is on duty as the floor-to-ceiling glass
wall facing the parking lot is shattered by a huge Brink's
armored truck that plows through and comes to a stop
virtually at the tellers' windows. The BANK OFFICIALS
and CUSTOMERS are in shock. The door to the truck
flies open and a masked figure clad in surgical attire jumps
out, holding a double barrel shotgun in one hand and an
automatic pistol in the other. It is Lomax, disguised as
Headhunter.

LOMAX
I've got my hands full so I'll need help
loading up.

The Security Guard reaches for his weapon and is blown
away.

LOMAX

Volunteers?

Two of the CUSTOMERS meekly raise their hands.

LOMAX

Empty the cash drawers and the vault. It's
all for a good cause—medical research.

HEAD TELLER

I know you—Headhunter!

LOMAX

I hope you carry Blue Cross.

Lomax shoots the legs out from under the teller. Everyone
else gasps. The two volunteers collect all the cash at an
accelerated pace.

LOMAX

Someday I'll find a cure for bullet
wounds. Toss the money in the back of
the truck—and get in along with it.

The volunteers hesitate a moment too long and Lomax
opens fire at their feet. The pair jump into the back of the
armored truck.

LOMAX

(to the others)
Now open wide, stick out your tongues
and say "AAAAH"!

All those at gunpoint open their mouths wide—as if being
examined—and say "AAAH" in unison.

LOMAX

I think you're all going to live. Just
remember if any of you decide to give
evidence against me, I still make house
calls.

Lomax climbs behind the wheel of the armored car and backs it up, spinning the wheel and driving straight through the bank and through the glass-enclosed front of the building onto the main street.

EXT. MAIN STREET—DAY

Police cars converge just as the armored car comes barreling out. Police open fire then flee for their lives as the armored car tries to run them down. Bank officials rush into the street shouting at the cops.

> OFFICIAL
> Hold your fire! He's taken hostages.

> 2ND OFFICIAL
> We know who it was!

CUT TO:

VIDEO SCREEN IN POLICE HEADQUARTERS

as LAW ENFORCEMENT OFFICIALS run and rerun the tape of what the video camera recorded in the bank. The FBI is represented in the group, which includes Det. Lt. Romero.

> ROMERO
> So much for all that humanitarian bullshit.

> FBI MAN
> Maybe the destruction of his laboratory
> pushed him off the deep end.

> 2ND FBI MAN
> Now he's looking to get revenge on
> society.

> HOGAN
> I don't care about his motives. That bank
> guard is dead! Find this sonofabitch and
> put him out of his misery!

INT. CABIN OF THE TUGBAOT—DAY

Ilona is reading the late edition of the newspaper which bears the headline: "HEADHUNTER KILLS BANK GUARD—LOOTS HALF MILLION."

Lomax watches her reaction to the article and the huge photograph on the front page taken by one of the bank's security cameras. The slightly blurred picture looks enough like the genuine Headhunter to be convincing. Ilona tosses the newspaper aside violently.

> LOMAX
>
> So your hero turns out to be a murderer and a thief.

> ILONA
>
> It must be because of me. I hurt him so deeply.

> LOMAX
>
> Now you're going to make excuses for him!

> ILONA
>
> No, you're right. I never knew him at all. (*beat*) Can you forgive me, Lomax.

> LOMAX
>
> First you've got to prove yourself. I've got a little something worked out for tonight that this city will never forget.

> ILONA
>
> Just tell me what you want me to do.

INT. KEN ARCHER'S HOME—NIGHT

As Ken stands in front of his projection television set watching news coverage of the robbery in which Headhunter shot a bank guard and escaped in an armored car. He's stunned by what he sees.

Then the doorbell rings. Ken stares at the front door terrified, as if expecting the police to break in. There's an insistent knock and then his SISTER'S VOICE.

                    MARGARET
          Ken! Let me in!

Ken finally unlocks the door and Margaret strides in.

                    MARGARET
          Were you expecting a S.W.A.T. team?

                    KEN
          Then you've seen it all on television.

                    MARGARET
          You don't remember doing it?

                    KEN
          Maggie, it wasn't me.

                    MARGARET
          A good attorney could argue that.

                    KEN
          No, I mean it really wasn't. I don't even
          have the damn uniform anymore.
          I ditched it in a junk yard.

                    MARGARET
          Your "alternate personality" could've
          gone back for it.

KEN

Look at the tape. You can see that's not me. The costume isn't even the same.

MARGARET

Then who is it?

KEN

If had to make a wild guess, I'd say Lomax.

MARGARET

Nobody's going to believe that.

KEN

Unless I catch him.

MARGARET

You? You're not equipped to go after someone like him.

KEN

I was before.

MARGARET

In your manic state.

KEN

A relapse would sure come in handy.

MARGARET

Unfortunately, relapses don't occur to order.

KEN

Have you got your car?

MARGARET

Right outside.

KEN

Come on then.

CUT TO:

EXT. CIRCULAR DRIVEWAY IN FRONT OF KEN'S
COLONIAL TYPE HOUSE—NIGHT

As Ken climbs into his sister's Mercedes. She's at the wheel.

MARGARET
Where to? Police headquarters?

KEN
Just drive.

She steps on the gas.

EXT. THE PARKWAY—NIGHT

Only scattered traffic as the Mercedes speeds along.

INT. THE MERCEDES—NIGHT

KEN
Take the next offramp.

MARGARET
Where the hell are we?

ANGLE ON THE RAMP

Leading to grim looking streets which surround the city
dump. On the far corner is a junkyard we have visited
before. The Mercedes pulls up at the warped looking fence
that surrounds the yard. Somewhere a dog is BARKING
wildly. Ken gets out and approaches the gate. Margaret
follows at a safe distance.

KEN
(shouts)
Anybody here?

The ELDERLY WATCHMAN approaches cautiously.

                    KEN
Do you remember me from the other
night?

                 WATCHMAN
What about it?

                    KEN
I left some belongings here. I need them
back. (*to Margaret*) Have you got a
hundred dollars on you?

                 MARGARET
The patient is supposed to pay me.

She reaches in her purse and comes up with the money.

                 WATCHMAN
I don't know if I can still find that stuff.

                    KEN
Try hard.

                                        CUT TO:

INT. STORAGE SHED, JUNKYARD—NIGHT

In the dim light the watchman wades through mounds of
old clothing that rise from floor to ceiling while Ken and
Margaret look on.

                 MARGARET
You believe this outfit will make the
difference?

                    KEN
They say clothes make the man.

                 WATCHMAN
Give me a hand. I think I got lucky.

Ken climbs up on the mountain of old clothes and helps dig
out what looks like the Headhunter wardrobe.

KEN

The cap and reflector have got to be here somewhere.

WATCHMAN

You mean that round shiny piece? I threw that in with the metal spare parts.

CUT TO:

EXT. THE JUNKYARD—NIGHT

Margaret waits impatiently out in the cold as Ken changes inside—into his alter ego. Finally he emerges, as Headhunter in full regalia.

MARGARET

Pardon me if I laugh. But now that I know it's you…

KEN

It doesn't seem to fit right anymore.

MARGARET

You'll get yourself shot on sight with that on.

KEN

Why can't I remember what it was like? Why can't I be "him" when I need to be?

MARGARET

Don't look at me like that. I can't help you.

KEN

Human blood. The sight of blood always triggered the transformation.

MARGARET

What do you want me to do? Bleed for you?

He motions her to the Mercedes and gets in. She joins him.

INT. THE MERCEDES—NIGHT

They ride together in silence. Closer now as brother and sister than they ever were before in their lives.

> MARGARET
> It won't work now, Ken. I changed you, just like you changed all those criminals.

> KEN
> I cured them of the obsession that made them outlaws… that streak of madness that I wish I had now. Maybe what I did was wrong after all.

> MARGARET
> If you're going to fight Lomax, it'll have to be as Ken Archer—mask or no mask.

Margaret's car phone rings. She answers it.

> MARGARET
> Yes, this is Dr. Archer.

> VOICE
> This is Dr. Powers speaking to you from King's Point Hospital.

> MARGARET
> At this hour? Is there some emergency?

> VOICE
> I take it you haven't been listening to your radio. Are you anywhere near the ferry terminal at Harbor Drive?

> MARGARET
> Ten, fifteen minutes away.

                    VOICE
They need all the trained medical
personnel they can get.

                  MARGARET
What's happened?

               DR. POWER'S VOICE
That madman, Headhunter, hijacked the
ferry. He threatens to sink the damn thing
with everyone aboard!

                  MARGARET
What can I do?

               DR. POWER'S VOICE
There are families of hostages down there
badly in need of psychiatric help. Report
to pier 12.

Margaret hangs up.

                  MARGARET
I know, little brother, pier 12.

                    KEN
How come we understand each other so
well all of a sudden?

                                        CUT TO:

EXT. PIER 12—NIGHT

DOZENS of police and emergency vehicles ring the
entrance of the pier. Tugboats and police launches are
loading up with armed officers garbed in bulletproof vests.
Members of the city's BOMB SQUAD suit up in their
protective gear. A makeshift hospital has been set up to the
left of the pier where the injured and wounded may receive
immediate attention.

Overhead POLICE HELICOPTERS hover, their searchlights casting a GHOSTLY ILLUMINATION over those who congregate below.

In the distance, well out in the harbor, the PASSENGER FERRY can be seen, immobilized and occupied by a madman who threatens the lives of the hundreds of innocents aboard. Representatives of the NEWS MEDIA linger beyond the police barricades, televising live coverage to the networks Ambulances are being allowed through. Margaret appears at the barricade with Ken carrying her medical bag. She flashes her ID.

MARGARET

Doctor Archer. This is my assistant. We're reporting to Doctor Powers.

OFFICER

Straight through there. Put these tags on.

The officer hands yellow tags to each of them which identify them as part of the task force. They are now free to move around inside the secured area. CAMERA FOLLOWS Ken and Margaret as they move to the far end of the pier where Mayor Keesley and Chief Hogan have set up a command post to direct these operations personally. We have met the mayor before at dinner at the Archer mansion. Margaret knows him quite well. Tonight he looks much the worse for wear. Right now he's on the ship-to-shore telephone with the man who's taken control of that ferry.

KEESLEY
(into phone)

Listen to me, Headhunter, if that's what you call yourself. We're willing to meet your terms.

VOICE ON PHONE

There was never any question of that!
I have the hull of the vessel wired with
plastic explosives. How many survivors

would there be in these freezing waters if
I pushed the detonator?

                    KEESLEY
There are seriously wounded people out
there who need to be evacuated. Then we
can talk...

                 VOICE ON PHONE
No one leaves the boat. You can send a
few medics out here but don't expect to
get them back.

The line goes dead. Keesley turns to Chief Hogan for advice.

                    HOGAN
I say we storm the boat. He's only one
man. I've got snipers up in the choppers
who can take him out if he steps out on
deck.

                    KEESLEY
Negative! We play it his way. Round up
medical volunteers right away.

Margaret steps forward and the mayor becomes aware of
her.

                    MARGARET
A female doctor wouldn't be as much of a
threat to him.

                    KEESLEY
But you're a psychiatrist, Margaret.

                    MARGARET
Exactly. Maybe I can calm him down.

                    HOGAN
Just set him up as a target for us. Lure him
out on the deck.

KEESLEY
If anything happens, your father will
never forgive me.

MARGARET
He'd never forgive me if I didn't go.

POLICE CAPTAIN
Follow me, doctors.

Margaret waves to Ken, who falls in beside her.

MARGARET
We're in. Although I don't know what
the hell you're going to do when we get
aboard.

KEN
Something will come to me.

CUT TO:

EXT. HARBOR SIDE, THE LAUNCH—NIGHT

FOUR MEDICS board the police launch along with
Margaret and Ken. The Police Captain waves to the captain
of the launch who pulls away from the pier, plowing through
choppy waters en route to the stranded ferry.

EXT. DECK OF FERRY—NIGHT

Strewn with the wounded, some of them transit police who
were shot when Lomax took control of the vessel over an
hour ago. They've lost a good deal of blood and medical
attention is overdue. Passengers try to perform basic first
aid. In the distance, the police launch draws closer. Lomax
is nowhere to be seen.

INT. CAPTAIN'S BRIDGE, THE FERRY—NIGHT

as Lomax holds the CAPTAIN, NAVIGATOR and FIRST
MATE at gunpoint. Lomax is completely masked, in a

costume that is a facsimile of Headhunter's. He also wears a flak jacket to which a number of remote detonators have been attached.

Lomax can set them off in an instant, if disobeyed. He peers out the window of the bridge and watches the arrival of the medical team.

> LOMAX
> Here come six more hostages.

The medical unit climbs aboard and begins tending the wounded on deck.

> LOMAX
> I'd better give them something to keep
> them busy.

He presses one of the detonator buttons.

ANGLE ON STARBOARD SIDE OF THE FERRY

A VAN which is parked along with dozens of other motor vehicles blows sky high. The force of the explosion smashes the windows of the passenger section of the ferry.

INT. PASSENGER SECTION—NIGHT

Passengers who are trapped aboard hug the floorboards and glass sprays everywhere. They're all afraid the ferry is about to sink. Life jackets are being distributed by crew members.

EXT. THE DECK—NIGHT

Ken and Margaret take cover from the explosion.

> MARGARET
> And you think you can stop him?

> KEN
> You've done all you can. Now it's up to
> me. Have faith.

He unbuckles the trenchcoat and flashes the Headhunter uniform at her quickly. He kisses his sister and quickly climbs the ladder leading to the upper deck.

EXT. UPPER DECK—NIGHT

Ken tries the door to a maintenance closet and slips inside.

HELICOPTER SHOT—NIGHT

Police choppers hover over the ferry with expert riflemen impatiently waiting for their target to give them a clear shot.

INT. THE BRIDGE—NIGHT

Lomax still holding the captain and crew at gunpoint.

> LOMAX
> How long will it take for this tub to sink
> after I blow a hole in the stern?

> CAPTAIN
> Depends on the size of the hole.

> LOMAX
> How about—this big?

He flicks another detonator button.

ANGLE ON STERN OF THE FERRY—NIGHT

From below the water line a massive explosion causes the ferry to list to the right.

ANGLE ON PIER

The Mayor and the Police Chief stare at the distant ferry— a portion of which is in flames.

> HOGAN
> He did it! The sonofabitch did it!

                              KEESLEY
                           (into intercom)
                All vessels converge and commence rescue
                operations. Get every private boat from
                the marina out there to help. People can't
                last five minutes in that water.

Cabin cruisers, yachts, motorized sailboats join the local
fishing fleet and the police and harbor patrol to surround
the floundering passenger ferry.

TIGHT ON ONE TUGBOAT

operated by a solitary woman. It is Ilona piloting the tug.

EXT. UPPER DECK, THE FERRY—NIGHT

Ken emerges from the storage closet clad now as
Headhunter. He heads up the metal ladder to the roof and
the ship's bridge, where Lomax has taken command.

HELICOPTER VIEW—ROOF OF FERRY—AS SEEN
FROM OVERHEAD

Headhunter can be seen running across the roof headed for
the bridge. The police snipers see him.

                           CHOPPER ONE
                Subject visible on roof above upper
                passenger deck.

                              SNIPER
                We read him. That's our man.

                           CHOPPER TWO
                We're going in.

ANGLE ON CHOPPER

as they swarm in for the kill. Headhunter is an easy target
up there. Machine guns open fire.

ANGLE ON HEADHUNTER

Zigzagging across the now tilting roof. The ferry is listing dramatically now. Bullets spray around Headhunter, who dives for cover beneath the steel ramp that provides direct access to the bridge.

AERIAL SHOT

The helicopters crisscrossing in an attack pattern, riddling the upper deck with bullets in an attempt to pick off the costumed man they have mistakenly identified as the hijacker of the ferry.

ANGLE ON KEN ARCHER AS HEADHUNTER

as the bullets ricochet all around him. Only the metal canopy overhead provides a shield.

ANGLE ON THE PASSENGER DECK

The ship's crew lowers lifeboats to the harbor and terrified passengers clamber in, a few losing their balance and toppling into the icy waters, only to be pulled out by others.

ANGLE ON DECK OF THE TUGBOAT ILONA

She maneuvers the craft around the marooned ferry drawing closer and closer.

INT. CAPTAIN'S BRIDGE, THE FERRY—NIGHT

Lomax wonders who the police have been shooting at.

> LOMAX
> Either they've got rotten aim or they're
> firing at somebody else.

Lomax reaches for the ship-to-shore telephone.

> LOMAX
> *(into phone)*
> This is Headhunter to Mayor Keesley. Call
> off the choppers or I'll detonate the charges.

EXT. PIER—NIGHT

The command center as the Mayor gets his instructions from the hijacker.

> KEESLEY
> I hear you loud and clear.

> LOMAX'S VOICE
> And keep those rescue boats away from
> my ferry. The passengers belong to me.

ANGLE ON THE UPPER DECK

CUT TO:

as the helicopters cease firing, make one final circle, then pull away from the vessel, giving Ken Archer a chance to emerge from cover and circle the captain's bridge.

INT. CAPTAIN'S BRIDGE

Lomax still on the ship-to-shore phone.

> LOMAX
> Now let's discuss the money, Mr. Mayor.
> How much per head?

At that moment, Ken Archer vaults through the window in the masked costume of Headhunter, diving straight at Lomax, who wears an almost identical outfit.

The captain and crew members are astounded to see two masked figures suddenly locked in mortal combat.

> LOMAX
> It took you long enough to get here.

Lomax retaliates, using his martial arts skills, techniques which Ken Archer may have mastered in his alter ego but which elude him now. Mentally he remains Ken Archer, cultivated and humane.

Lomax whirls, aiming a karate kick at Ken's chest which connects hard, propelling him backward, smashing him through the door to the captain's bridge and out onto the metal platform some 20 feet above the upper deck.

Lomax lunges after him and the two men exchange blows. Ken is almost knocked over the rail but hangs on, swinging back up and catching Lomax with both feet just beneath the jaw.

It is Lomax who plunges over the rail, landing 20 feet below on the roof of the upper deck. It is a glass roof crisscrossed with steel girders. The dome cracks but does not collapse.

Before Lomax can get to his feet, Ken Archer dives down, landing on top of him and knocking the wind out of him.

INT. CAPTAIN'S BRIDGE—NIGHT

The Captain reaches in a drawer and finds a service revolver. He runs out on a metal platform above ready to shoot someone.

HIS POV

The two masked figures fighting below. ANGLE ON THE CAPTAIN

He doesn't know which one to shoot.

ANGLE ON THE HELICOPTERS

Circling back.

INT. CHOPPER—NIGHT

> AERIAL GUNNER
> I can see them both now. I can get a clear shot.

PILOT
Them?

AERIAL GUNNER
There are two of them now.

PILOT
(over radio)
Charlie to Control. Request permission
to fire!

ANGLE ON THE UPPER DECK

As Ken Archer and Lomax continue their life and death
struggle. CAMERA TILTS UP to the approaching
helicopters drawing ever closer. Lomax and Ken are sitting
ducks. They will be easily dispatched by the first volley of
fire.

CUT TO:

EXT. COMMAND POST ON PIER—NIGHT

The Mayor and Chief Hogan listening to the report from
the choppers.

HOGAN
I don't care how many there are. Take
them out!

KEESLEY
Commence firing!

CUT TO:

ANGLE ON LOMAX AND KEN

Fighting on the curved glass dome of the ferry as the glass
beneath them begins to collapse.

And now just as the helicopters open fire, the surface beneath
Ken and Lomax caves in and they both plummet out of sight,
the machine gun spray missing them by mere seconds.

INT. PASSENGER SECTION, THE FERRY

As Lomax and Ken tumble to the floor of the passenger section which is deserted. All of the passengers have rushed out on deck to save themselves.

Lomax springs to his feet and goes after Ken, who is still stunned.

But Ken has been playing possum. As Lomax leans over, Ken connects and then follows up with a barrage of punches.

One blow strikes Lomax in the chest, hitting one of the detonators on that remote control vest.

The punch causes one of the explosives on the ferry to detonate.

Ken has inadvertently set off the charge himself.

The ferry lurches sharply. Both men are thrown off their feet.

> LOMAX
> Throw a few more like that and you'll
> sink the boat yourself.

Lomax comes for Ken, who is now virtually afraid to throw a punch lest he inadvertently set off still another explosion.

Lomax reaches inside his uniform and withdraws a small snub-nose revolver. Now Lomax is armed while Ken has only his bare hands and his wits.

As Lomax opens fire, Ken drops out of range down a spiral staircase into the boiler room below, which is already ablaze.

INT. BOWELS OF THE SHIP—NIGHT

Ken dodges bullets from above as he drops into the flaming boiler room.

The furnaces have been flooded and the oil-soaked boiler room is like a huge bomb ready to go off. Then it erupts in a burst of fire. Ken is swallowed up by the inferno.

EXT. THE DECK—NIGHT

Assuming Ken to be dead, Lomax races out of the passenger section. CAMERA FOLLOWING him onto the shielded portion of the deck where dozens of cars are parked for the voyage across the bay. He selects one particular minibus parked at the very tip of the vessel.

He unhooks the chain that provides the only obstacle to prevent such a vehicle from driving straight off the ferry into the bay.

ANGLE ON THE OTHER SIDE OF DECK—NIGHT

where the passengers are again being rescued. The hijacker has lost control of the vessel and the rescue party is making the most of the opportunity. There's a virtual fleet of rescue boats clustered around the ferry. There have been no more explosions to inhibit the evacuation. One of the evacuees is Margaret, who tends to the wounded among them.

ANGLE ON ILONA'S TUGBOAT

as she steers it to the far side of the ferry, toward the very tip of the vessel.

ANGLE ON LOMAX

as he catches sight of the tugboat with Ilona on deck. Before she can catch sight of him, Lomax slips out of the Headhunter costume and tosses it aside. He still doesn't want her to know he's been posing at Headhunter.

ANGLE ON LOMAX

as he gets behind the wheel of the minibus and starts the ignition. He intends to drive the vehicle off the ferry into the water.

ANGLE ON ILONA

Releasing the towline and the huge hook, which is attached to a winch powerful enough to tow a freighter through the harbor.

ANGLE ON THE FRONT OF THE MINIBUS

The huge bumper around which the hook will fit so neatly.

That has been their escape plan. Lomax will drive off the ferry in the minibus which will float long enough for Ilona to secure the towline, then the tug will tow the minibus safely across the bay. A masterful escape.

CLOSE-UP—LOMAX

CAMERA DROPPING to his foot as it presses the gas pedal.

ANGLE ON THE WHEELS OF THE MINIBUS

as it begins to move forward to the very edge of the ferry. In a moment it will plunge into the icy waters.

INT. MINIBUS ALREADY IN MOTION—NIGHT

It will drop some 20 feet through the air into the churning water. All at once the opposite door flies open and Ken jumps in beside Lomax. His face and clothing are stained dark with slicks of oil but he has emerged from the inferno below decks with only minor injuries.

He seizes the wheel, struggling with Lomax in an attempt to stop the vehicle.

WIDE ANGLE SHOT—THE DECK OF THE FERRY—NIGHT

as the van springs forward and plummets off the edge of the ferry into the cold black water.

ANGLE ON ILONA ON THE TUGBOAT

backing in still closer to the ferry, ready to make contact with the van and hook on the winch line. She doesn't realize that Ken is inside that vehicle as well and that he and Lomax are struggling to the death.

INT. THE MINIBUS—NIGHT

which is tipped over on its side. The door on the passenger side is still open and the seawater is pouring in filling up the vehicle.

Ordinarily it would float for minutes. Being empty and airtight it would have a natural buoyancy. This is what Lomax was counting on.

But with Ken's intervention and the open passenger door, the front of the vehicle is becoming heavy and is tipping under water.

The very place where Ilona was to attach the towline is now inaccessible.

WIDE ANGLE SHOT—THE MINIBUS

as the current sweeps it away from the ferry which is a scene of absolute chaos as the rescues continue.

Ilona's tugboat backs up in pursuit but the car is submerging, going under.

UPSIDE DOWN SHOT INSIDE MINIBUS

Lomax and Ken again locked in combat.

Then the water rises above them, and they are both struggling to hold their breath.

ANGLE ON LOMAX'S HAND

as he forces the door on his side open. The water pressure is against him but he manages to struggle through.

EXT. MINIBUS UNDER WATER

as Lomax wiggles out of the vehicle which is upside down and sinking rapidly.

ANGLE ON KEN

Left inside, raising his feet and kicking out the windshield.

ANGLE ON THE WATER'S SURFACE, THE BAY— NIGHT

as Lomax breaks the surface. The light of a helicopter sweeps past, its searchlights passing over the water in search of survivors. There are other survivors out there bobbing around in their yellow life jackets.

Lomax swims toward one such survivor. A MIDDLE-AGED MAN struggling to stay afloat, kept alive only by the buoyancy of that yellow jacket.

But Lomax wants that life jacket. He reaches the man, pulls him under brutally, and strips the jacket off the thrashing figure. It is not Lomax's intention to perish in these treacherous currents.

ANGLE ON KEN

Seeing what's happening, he begins swimming to the rescue of the victim.

Both he and Lomax have been swept far away from the sinking ferry, far away from Ilona's tugboat.

ANGLE ON ILONA

Her keen eyes skimming the surface of the water. She has lost sight of the van which has sunk. She can't find any trace of Lomax.

> ILONA
> *(screaming)*
> Lomax! Lomax! Where are you?

ANGLE FAR OUT IN THE BAY—NIGHT

Lomax attempting to drown the victim and take his life jacket. Then all at once he is seized from behind in a choke hold and pulled under by Ken.

The hapless victim swims away as fast as possible clinging to that precious yellow life jacket.

OVERHEAD SHOT

The two men struggling as a helicopter passes overhead and drops flares into the water to assist the harbor patrol in finding those still afloat out there in the darkness.

ANGLE ON THE WATER'S SURFACE

A flare falls close to Lomax and Ken. Lomax reaches out with his gloved hand, seizes the burning flare and attempts to blind Ken with it. Ken's oil-soaked clothing catches fire and he disappears below the surface.

ANGLE ON LOMAX

as he begins to swim furiously toward the outline of the tugboat. He hears Ilona's voice calling to him.

HIS POV FROM WATER LEVEL

The tugboat is backing up swiftly.

ANGLE ON ILONA

as she spots him and reaches out for him.

ANGLE ON LOMAX

as he is pulled aboard, exhausted but safe.

                         LOMAX
            Gun that engine. Let's go.

Ilona switches the throttle to the forward position and the tugboat moves off at top speed. The towline is still straggling out behind it.

ANGLE ON KEN

Swimming in the water, then seizing the towline just as the tugboat pulls away. Ken is towed along in the darkness.

Wherever Lomax is going, Ken will be there too.

MOVING SHOT CROSSING THE BAY

The tugboat speeding along. In the far background the last remains of the passenger ferry as it sinks beneath the surface. Around it, dozens of rescue boats, the night sky crowded with choppers with their crisscrossing searchlights beaming down.

The surface of the water ablaze with flares.

ANGLE ON LOMAX ABOARD THE TUGBOAT

Ilona is drying him off when she notices remnants of the costume he had been wearing: the steel wristbands and the medical utility belt that she is so familiar with.

ILONA
You were dressed like him weren't you?
You wanted him to be blamed.

LOMAX
I didn't want you to find that out until
after we had time to celebrate.

ILONA
The robbery at the bank. That was you!

LOMAX
I had to get you back on my side.

                    ILONA
      And you talk about having a sense of honor!

                    LOMAX
      Say a prayer for the good doctor and then
      forget him.

                    ILONA
      You mean he's dead?

                    LOMAX
      I cooked him and fed him to the sharks.
      Pull into that cove.

WIDER ANGLE ON THE TUGBOAT

as it slows down and turns into a small cove near a fishing
village.

ANGLE ON KEN

still being towed behind the tugboat. As the tugboat comes
to a halt, Ken releases the towline and swims closer to the
tug.

ANGLE ON DECK OF THE TUG

Ilona fights her way free as Lomax attempts to take her in
his arms.

                    ILONA
      Just go away, Lomax.

                    LOMAX
      He's still got your brain scrambled.

                    ILONA
      No. He's not making me do this. I'm
      doing it on my own!

He realizes she's holding a gun on him. When he advances
toward her, she fires a shot at his feet. She means business.

LOMAX
So he's dead, but he wins after all.

Then, without warning, Lomax is whirled around and Ken connects with a left hook to Lomax's jaw that sends him sprawling. Ken is dripping wet, having just climbed aboard.

KEN
You didn't bother to send flowers.

ILONA
(to Ken)
You really do have a very nice face.

Ilona extends the gun to Ken.

ILONA
Here, you better take this.

KEN
No. I want you to turn him in yourself.
You'll get a lot of points for that at the
trial.

ILONA
You're not going to try to cure me again?

KEN
You've already cured yourself. I think
that's the only way it really works.

At that moment, Lomax leaps up and Ken clobbers him again, sending him sprawling at Ilona's feet.

KEN
I'm getting better at this.

Now, Ken steps ashore onto the dock, leaving Ilona in control of the boat, with Lomax at gunpoint.

ILONA
You're not leaving me alone with him?

KEN

If he moves, just wound him a little.

ILONA

When will I see you?

KEN

You don't need me anymore.

The silence is broken by the scream of a POLICE SIREN.

THEIR POV

Two police launches with red lights beaming heading toward the dock carrying survivors, but also carrying armed police who will certainly take Lomax into custody. Romero is identifiable among the cops.

ANGLE ON THE TUGBOAT AT THE DOCK

KEN

Fire another round. That'll bring them
quicker!

Ilona fires a shot in the air then trains the gun back on Lomax who has again started to edge forward.

ILONA

Which kneecap do you think is best?

KEN

Your choice.

Lomax backs off. He believes she will indeed shoot him.

Ken has already vanished into the fog that is sweeping in across this inlet, a fog that already reflects the red glow of the lights of the police launches as they now sweep in on either side of the tugboat.

ANGLE ON LT. ROMERO AND HARBOR POLICE

Jumping onto the dock and running to the tugboat, stopping short as he realizes that it is Ilona and that she has a prisoner.

> ILONA
> Hello again, lieutenant. You remember Lomax.

Ilona hands Romero the gun.

> ROMERO
> I'd like to give you a big kiss, but I'm on duty.

> ILONA
> When do you get off?

> ROMERO
> I thought you were in love with Headhunter.

> ILONA
> There really isn't any such person. Lomax made him up. You can see he's still got part of the costume on.

The wrist bands, the boots.

> ROMERO
> How about it, Lomax? Is that true? Been living a double life?

> LOMAX
> *(laughs)*
> Ilona isn't capable of telling lies anymore. You know that. Sure, I'm Headhunter. Why not?

> ROMERO
> Read him his rights and get him out of here.

The policemen haul Lomax off of the tug and disappear down the dock with their prisoner securely handcuffed. Romero helps Ilona off the vessel, takes off his jacket, and wraps it around her shoulders to keep her warm.

                    ROMERO
          It could be embarrassing if our medical
          friend ever turned up again.

                    ILONA
     He won't.

                    ROMERO
     Are you warm enough?

                    ILONA
     Yes. Thanks.

They begin to walk off now. Romero holds her protectively, affectionately.

                    ROMERO
     Oh, before I forget... you're under arrest.

                    ILONA
     I knew you were going to say that.

                                        DISSOLVE TO:

INT. MARGARET'S BROWNSTONE—NIGHT

as she returns home, worried and forlorn. Something has happened to her brother and she's not sure what. She switches on the lights to find Ken asleep on her living room couch.

                    MARGARET
          Well, you've had me worried sick. How
          did you get in here?

                    KEN
     I picked the lock. You know how handy I am.

MARGARET
They caught Headhunter. Do you know
who it turned out to be? (*beat*) Lomax,
after all.

KEN
What a surprise.

MARGARET
They managed to save almost all the
passengers. I spent all night treating them
for shock and worrying about you.

KEN
How about some eggs and bacon? Can
you cook?

MARGARET
I never learned how.

Ken walks to the window and looks out at the city in the
distance.

There across the river stretches the vast skyline of Central
City, USA.

MARGARET
Apparently Ilona is the hero of the day.
(*beat*) You're going to miss her.

KEN
I think she was way too tall for me.

MARGARET
So what's next for Ken Archer?

KEN
I guess the sight of blood doesn't bother
me too much anymore.

MARGARET
So?

KEN

So I think I'll go back to medical school
and make dad proud.

MARGARET

You could be one helluva brain surgeon.

KEN

Or maybe I'll come up with a new
"specialty" of my own.

MARGARET

I'm sure.

EXT. ANGLE ON KEN AND HIS SISTER MARGARET

standing at the window together, looking out at the city
as CAMERA begins to pull away (AS SHOT FROM
HELICOPTER). As we draw away from them we SWEEP
up over the city, a city where the name of Headhunter has
been whispered for many months.

Now he has ceased to exist and Ken Archer's life will
begin again. Free from the trauma of his childhood, he is
nonetheless too unique an individual to be "just another
doctor." Perhaps the phantom physician is not completely
gone after all. Perhaps Headhunter will return to again
capture and cure those who threaten our society.

For now this adventure is over.

FADE OUT

THE END.

www.ingramcontent.com/pod-product-compliance
Lightning Source LLC
Chambersburg PA
CBHW060436130626
46555CB00005B/2375

979 8 8 9 9 7 6 0 3 2 7